ROMANCING THE BEAN

ESSENTIALS FOR CREATING VEGETARIAN BEAN DISHES

Joanne Saltzman
Author of *Amazing Grains*

H J Kramer Inc
Tiburon, California

Dedicated to my late friend
Martha Keyes

H J Kramer Inc
P.O. Box 1082
Tiburon, CA 94920

Library of Congress Cataloging-in-Publication Data

Saltzman, Joanne, 1948–
    Romancing the bean : essentials for creating vegetarian bean
dishes / Joanne Saltzman.
        p.   cm.
    ISBN 0–915811–48–0 (pbk.) : $12.95
    1. Cookery (Beans)   2. Vegetarian cookery.   I. Title.
TX803.B4S25   1993
641.6′565 — dc20   93–1828
                                                              CIP

Editor: Jay Harlow
Cover Design and Art: Tina Cash
Book Illustrations: Vicki Lee Johnston
Editorial Assistants: Nancy Grimley Carleton and Claudette Charbonneau
Book Production: Schuettge and Carleton
Typesetting: Classic Typography
Manufactured in the United States of America
10 9 8 7 6 5 4 3 2 1

Books by Joanne Saltzman

*Amazing Grains: Creating Vegetarian
Main Dishes With Whole Grains*

*Romancing the Bean: Essentials for
Creating Vegetarian Bean Dishes*

THANKS

Of the many people involved in seeing this project through, I want to thank Jay Harlow, my editor, for his great sense of humor and terrific skill with cooking and writing, and especially for his ability to understand the process and the scope of my vision.

Appreciation for Linda and Hal Kramer, my publishers, who recognize the potential healing available from my work, and particularly for supporting a thorough recipe testing.

Deep gratitude to Lynn Milot, who opened her beautiful home to make the bean party a most exotic and memorable experience. To Colleen Miller, who graced us with her humor, and to Scott Die and my children, Maia, Joey, Jake, and Ryan, who ran errands and provided the muscle for cleanup and setup. And a bounty of thanks goes to the courageous people who cooked, having to follow a recipe even though I had trained some of them not to, and to their friends and family who evaluated samples of more beans than anyone should eat at one time; and thanks to the people who wanted to come and couldn't. Among the many who helped are: Lotus Walker, Shasha Immerman, John Gritton, Nona Nading, Alison Litchfield, Cathy Daly, Kristen Wilson, Shelly Zucker, Josh and Marta Bean, Carrie Wagner, Nieca Coombs, Carl and Avi Sternberg, Kathleen O'Brien, Steve Wiener, Sheri Irby, Peggy Markel, P. J. Sherman, Jim and Susan Tremaine, Jo Ellen Mazula, Karen Cargnel, Joyce Gordon, Christina Rosa, Robin Claire, and Taulere Appel.

More special thanks go to Vicki Lee Johnston for the artful illustrations; Susan Van Auken for sending me exotic beans to play with; Harriet Chorney for the use of her Crockpot among other things; Martha Morvan for explaining the nutritional dynamics of the ingredients; and to Linda Hubbly, Mary Bowman, and Trise Cruea for endless support.

I am extremely grateful to Eden Foods, who sent many cooked beans (already first-stage cooked) to expedite inventions; and to Ivy Foods, who generously shared their extraordinary vegetable protein product to accompany beans.

CONTENTS

Part III. Tofu and Tempeh Cookery

Appendix

Recipes by Bean
ANASAZI, BOLITA, PINTO

AZUKI

BLACK TURTLE

Introduction

When I shared the title of this book with friends, their responses startled me. Laughter and pain were the main reactions. A dear friend claimed, with a glint of laughter in her eye, "It's a lot of work to romance my husband after he eats beans." And a realtor halted, recalling passing memories of somewhat embarrassing and painful stomach aches.

It has taken me a while to laugh fully at the humorous side of bean eating, realizing that I have always regarded beans more as royalty than as jesters. Beans are extremely powerful. They participate in healing the ecology of our planet and maintaining the health of the human body. They even give a boost to one's pocketbook because usually they are inexpensive.

I want to suggest two things to people who are timid about eating beans. One, if beans are not thoroughly cooked, I would not eat them either. There are very few restaurants (other than Mexican) that serve beans that are cooked well enough to avoid digestive problems. And I'm sorry to say, I haven't seen many properly cooked beans from well-intentioned cooks either. Two, when beans are cooked properly, they are so seductive, we usually overeat them. This also becomes a digestive problem. So I want to encourage you to have your body build a relationship with bean eating slowly. Over perhaps a year, your body will tolerate a higher amount. And then you should still be careful on quantity of intake.

Romancing the Bean is intended to share technical information about the variety of dried beans and how to cook them so you can experience their sensuality and versatility. They have taken me into extraordinary culinary adventures. After eating beans at least once a day for several months while developing these recipes, I received more than an invitation to a love affair with a brave, honest, and heroic food group; I found the humor that until now the rest of the world enjoyed without me.

Beans, second to grains as the most important food group, fit neatly on a plate with grain dishes. Together, grains and beans offer us the full complement of amino acids, allowing us to obtain complete protein from plants. To those who have read my previous book *Amazing Grains,* as well as to new readers, I am delighted to share some very special bean recipes with you. I really see the two books as a set, and I will frequently refer you to *Amazing Grains* for companion dishes and to further your understanding of ingredients. In both books, serving suggestions with each dish offer complete meal ideas based on a dairy-free and animal-free diet.

Like *Amazing Grains,* this is two books in one. The recipes provide examples of the cooking methods; but more important, think of this book as a guide to creativity in making your own bean dishes. The creative process that I teach with food and cooking (see the Creative Process chapter) empowers you in many ways.

My intent is to distill the language of chefs — a way to communicate about dishes that embraces the thoughts behind putting them together. Every dish in any recipe book or at any restaurant can be looked at in terms of the creative process. As you begin to identify dishes in this manner, you will expand your repertoire and the magnificent possibilities for creating your own dishes.

Don't be afraid to make mistakes when substituting ingredients in a recipe or inventing a visionary dish, because those mistakes, if indeed they should ever occur, teach you more than a good recipe could ever teach you. The "process" part of each recipe describes some of the reasons the ingredients were chosen. The worksheet guides you through the process. Study the ingredients, their function and character, and the cooking method descriptions. Then put the three together, inventing your own dishes on the spot with foods at hand.

The sample recipes in this book are both romantic and practical. When you follow them, you will find that they will be much more delicious if you pay attention to your common sense and sensory facilitators, especially smell, taste, and vision. These recipes have been tested thoroughly, but you still need to have *intention* and *attention* toward what you are making. These secret ingredients embellish every dish. They are not available in the markets and no one can give them to you.

These dishes are simple, often not including more than five ingredients. Each one counts. I can't impress upon you enough the importance of choosing quality ingredients. The most remarkable comment I can share with you from the recipe testing is that occasionally the taste of a dish was altered just enough to be frustrating due to the quality of ingredients that were used. For example, one time the chili powder used was old and had no "umph" so the dish seemed flat. Another time, a less potent sea salt was used and the dish did not harmonize. (The sea salt that I use is four times stronger than regular salt.) If you are inclined to follow a recipe exactly, I encourage you either to locate the same ingredients used in this book or to pay attention to the taste process. Watch for the integration of taste. As you do, you can adapt the amounts according to the quality of your ingredients and the strength of your personality. You see, most of these recipes are fairly mild because I don't like spicy food (although the more I teach, the spicier and bolder I become). There is no reason for you not to increase the dosage of spices to satisfy your tastes.

When you are eating these bean dishes, the longer you take to chew and savor the flavor, the better you will feel from eating them. Unlike meat, the initial taste of a bean dish is not always an instant gratification. But also unlike meat, the longer you chew and let the flavors and texture play in your mouth, the more dramatic and enjoyable the experience. Romance the bean, and it will definitely love you back. That includes treating it with respect, handling it appropriately, and not overindulging.

Even the most organized cook sometimes has to improvise on short notice. Use Eden brand canned beans for shortcuts. Eden Foods has taken care in the preparation of its canned beans to make them more digestible than other brands.

Thank you for your letters about *Amazing Grains.* I am pleased that you have found "the process" useful. Please continue to write and inquire about the School of Natural Cookery (see page 170). We created the SNC Products catalogue so that you can find special ingredients and cookware. And some of you may be interested in teaching this process in your area.

Joanne

Part I
The Noble Bean

A Powerful Food

Romance in cooking is hardly new. Sharing love through food is a primal experience that can be rekindled at any time. Yes, even with beans. Beans have been laughed at, considered low-class food ("poor man's meat"), and been the brunt of numerous digestion jokes. Yet I imagine if beans could talk, their point of view would sound like this:

> And Queen Bean said to the little seedlings, "Why are we not honored at the table of fast-food dwellers? Why is not our glory seen in the kingdom of their plates?" She proceeded to sway her audience with smooth words, thick with intensity, and speckled with humor. "Our integrity is unmatched; our form noble, elliptical, reflecting shapes of the universe, sometimes matching the shape of human organs. We build and rebuild the very fiber of a cell into a grand muscle. There is not a drop of excess useless waste from our kind. Each part of our life—our stalk, our flowers, and our seed—is given to humanity. Our sweet taste and velvet touch receive the company of seasonings may they be hot, sweet, or aromatic. We do not judge. We receive, with open heart, flavors of the world. But beware we're not the jester. Mistreat us and there could be suffering. Ignore the essence of our being and we will fight back, causing internal agony. But care for us as you would your loved ones and we give our bounty: nourishment for the body and peace for the spirit. For when you take us as food, no animal will suffer."

Beans Through History

Beans are among the oldest foods cultivated by humanity. We read in Genesis that Esau was a "cunning hunter," but when he was hungry he sold his birthright to his brother Jacob for bread and "pottage of lentils." Older cultures have counted heavily on bean cuisine, especially in combination with grain. Oriental combinations use the soybean with barley and rice; traditional American people ate a wide variety of colorful beans with colorful corn; India brings *dal* and rice together; Mediterraneans eat chick-peas with wheat in the form of couscous, bulgur, pasta, and pita bread; and Ethiopian culture serves injera bread with crushed peas and lentils. It is only fairly recently and in the industrialized West that beans have been used mainly in combination with meat, as a vegetable rather than a basic source of protein. Perhaps North America will soon acknowledge the power of this simple food.

Travel and trade have disguised the original sources in many cases, but modern archaeology has traced beans as part of the diet of humanity to the prehistoric era, back at least 15,000 years ago. As early as 2,000 B.C., history records that beans were rotated with grain to benefit the soil. All legume plants (beans and peas) absorb nitrogen from the air and fix it in the soil, replenishing an element necessary to all plant growth. This practice of using bean plants as "green manure" is still important today throughout the world.

Beans also took part in superstition and ritual. The Greeks fostered a belief that beans held the souls of dead men, and to walk across a bean field was sacrilege. Both the Greeks and Romans used beans as a symbol when casting votes for political office and for trial verdicts; a white bean signified a yes vote or deemed a man innocent, and black beans voted him out of office or found him guilty (the source of today's term "blackballing").

Southwest American Zuni initiated young men about twelve years old into the *kiva* (a spiritual meeting place, usually round and underground) by having them bring a bowl of boiled beans in the color that represented the *kiva* they were entering. This ritual encouraged the cultivation of many varieties of beans, what modern science calls "maintaining genetic diversity." Hopi priests break ritual fasts by eating beans, and some people use a Mexican custom of placing three beans on their temples to relieve a headache. Beans found in tombs high in the South American Andes mountains reveal their position in a pre-Inca civilization. The beans were stored in clay pots decorated with designs of men and women holding an ear of corn in one hand and a bean stalk in the other. This traditional relationship of beans and corn demonstrates a marriage of foods supporting each other nutritionally and organically as they grow entwined from the earth to the sky, the gentle bean wrapped around the sturdy cornstalk.

Categories of Beans

Today there are over 1,000 different varieties of beans. How you classify them may have something to do with you. A gardener looks at botanical names, growing habits (pole or bush varieties), and sometimes climate. A historian looks to the origins and journeys of beans, contrasting Mediterranean broad beans and lentils with Asian soybeans and common beans from the Americas. Culinary artists regard shape, color, size, and flavor. But to me, the most important factor in classifying beans is the cooking time that they require. As new (old) beans appear, and they will, it is important to know how to make them digestible. Knowing their cooking requirements could be as simple as classifying them into short-, medium-, or long-cooking beans.

Short-cooking beans, such as lentils, mung beans, and azuki beans, are usually small and can have a larger carbohydrate component than medium- or long-cooking beans. They take less time than medium or long-cooking beans to reach a satisfying smoothness in the first-stage cooking method (see page 16). Often they are split, the category known as *dal* in Indian cooking, which includes red lentils or split peas.

Medium-cooking beans are the most common kind of bean. Black turtle, kidney, pinto, and navy are just a few. When you encounter a new bean, test it as a medium-cooking bean. If it is still hard after the first-stage method, you will know that it really belongs in the long-cooking category.

Long-cooking beans, such as garbanzo and soybean, require long soaking, whereas medium-cooking beans may or may not need to be soaked, depending on the strength of the stomachs that will be eating them and the first-stage cooking method that is followed.

Beans in the Body

From a nutritional point of view, beans provide mostly protein with some complex carbohydrates. Protein, the nutrient that maintains the body, building and rebuilding most tissue, is the fundamental material of all plants and animals, and dietary protein is essential to survival. Although there is protein in grain, beans are the most important source of protein in the plant world.

Only recently, beginning with the studies of William C. Rose in the 1940s and 50s, has the chemistry of protein been researched. Proteins are strings of amino acids, of which there are twenty-some varieties; half of them are constructed by the body from the elements already in the body, but the rest must come from the diet. Meat, eggs, and milk products offer enough amino acid combinations for each to be a complete protein. Beans and grains are both high in protein, but neither one offers complete protein by itself; put them together, however, and the combination of essential amino acids is complete.

Unfortunately, protein consumption has become a bit of an obsession, obvious in plates of food that measure 75 percent meat, 20 percent starch, and 5 percent vegetables. Quantity of protein has some-

"We need protein in our food because it constitutes the basic machinery of all life. Proteins are at the heart of all organic movement, change and growth: the most important characteristics of life itself."

Harold McGee
On Food and Cooking

Proteins are chemicals. Give your body a few to inspire it, and it will make more.

how gotten mixed up with quality. Fortunately, vegetable protein performs more efficiently in the body than animal protein, and it usually comes with much less fat attached. It also offers equal, if not more, opportunity for culinary pleasure.

DIGESTING BEANS

Beans have a notorious reputation for being difficult to digest. Science has come to some understanding of this situation, pointing to a group of carbohydrate molecules called *oligosaccharides*. But from the research that I have done into the science of food and cooking, the answer to the poor digestibility of beans lies mostly with the secondary compounds. If you have ever given birth to a baby or an idea, you know the strength of our creative forces; not just a passion, but a downright vicious defense mechanism works to protect our offspring. Beans rely on secondary compounds (protease inhibitors, lectin, and cyanogen) to defend the parts of the plant that are essential for reproduction, the seed and the shoot (sprout). As these compounds defend the bean they interfere with the digestive process, sometimes demanding a need for more energy (to create enough enzymes to digest the bean) than the nutrition earned from eating it. Cooking is the only way to conquer the bean's defense; fire drives off the secondary compounds, making the bean digestible.

There are two secrets to preventing an intestine-bean attack. One, cook beans thoroughly. Why fight the reproductive forces of nature if cooking breaks down these indigestible compounds? Eat beans that are partially cooked and you are asking for trouble. Two, don't eat too many. Each body has its limits in the quantity of beans it can handle.

Environmental Benefits of Beans

Consider the environmental benefits of eating beans. Simply stated, if more people increase their intake of vegetable protein, fewer animals will have to be raised, and more land will be available for growing plants. In his book *Beyond Beef: The Rise and Fall of the Cattle Culture,* Jeremy Rifkin cites statistical data that affront one's common sense:

> We could feed one billion more people if we used land
> to grow food rather than feed. . . . The cattle industry poses
> an unprecedented threat to the global environment, to human
> health, and to the economic stability of our civilization. Cattle

are a major cause of world hunger, pollution, deforestation, and desertification, and they play a central role in the extinction of wild species. In addition they produce vast amounts of methane, a key factor in global warming. Cattle literally threaten the future of the earth.

You don't have to be a vegetarian to help the planet. Even if you add meat to your bean dishes, it's a more efficient source of protein than meat alone, and it helps cut down on the massive animal consumption dominant in this century. Beans, grains, and vegetables have supported many people through the ages. Our future depends on getting back to a more earth-friendly, plant-based diet. Mother Earth can give many seeds from one plant. Those seeds returning to the earth bear again and again. When you eat plant protein, you help balance the animal protein in your body and on the earth. Embrace a simple shift of quantities. Bring more plants into your life. You literally will be eating earth, becoming one with earth's power, and you will have the ability to hear her needs.

The Creative Process

The more I work with the creative process and watch how other people use it, the more I am impressed with the power it has to change people's lives. This process brings your spirit to your creation, and your cooking becomes an expression of you. By using it, we can assemble meals quickly, respond to any dietary concern, and watch personalities and consciousness evolve.

The creative process in cooking is a delicate balance between the theory and technique of cooking and messages from the senses of taste, smell, touch (texture), and sight (color). When I truly follow a recipe, measuring accurately and following the steps, I give up all creativity and have to trust someone else's instincts. It becomes a way to install the theory of cooking into the logical part of the brain, but it is potentially dangerous. Just cooking from theory, relying on the logical part of the brain (the left side), excludes a vast information bank of what is appropriate. Knowledge stored in the intuitive part of the brain (the right side) is referenced from a part of us that carries deep memories from the beginning of the soul's journey. These memories are about survival, good things, dreams and ambitions, and not so good things.

The right brain is programmed to live in harmony with the spirit. Unlike choices made from the left side of the brain, choices made from this deep sensory awareness cannot be harmful. In fact, often they are healing.

Creativity in cooking can be generated from three separate situations: one, when an unlimited selection of ingredients is available and the cook can apply theories of color, taste, texture, and the energetic balance of ingredients and cooking methods; another, when the pantry is sparse and the cook fashions a meal highlighting perhaps only one or two ingredients; and the third, from sheer passion and a driving desire for a special taste, ingredient, or dish. Whichever way you enter the preparation, you can trust that your intuitive right brain will not hurt you. Instead, by using it, you enhance your whole life.

Theory is where you will store information on how salt is used, whether a dish is covered or not, how to know when beans are fully cooked, and so on. Even though this information will determine the success of a dish, it is the other side, the intuitive part of the brain, that selects which and how much salt, herbs, spices, accent liquid, and other ingredient choices you use.

Here, one's *attention* and *intention* become critical. Paying attention to the transformation and alchemical changes of the food and having an intention of making a good dish are essential elements of cooking

DECORATIVE VEGETABLES CHART

YELLOW-ORANGE
Sweet yellow peppers
Yellow summer squash
Corn
Carrots
Winter squash
Sweet potatoes
Nasturtium flowers

RED-PURPLE
Sweet red peppers
Red radishes
Tomatoes
Red onions
Purple cabbage
Beets

GREEN
Peas
Green beans
Green onions
Zucchini
Green peppers
Celery
Leafy greens
Green olives
Artichoke hearts

WHITE
White onions
Fennel (anise)
Belgian endive
Cauliflower
Hearts of palm
Daikon (white radish)
Bean sprouts
Water chestnuts

BLACK
Burdock root
Black olives
Black sesame seeds

that come alive when using the creative process. These secret ingredients almost guarantee success and are not found in recipes or in grocery stores.

Theories of energetics, color, taste, and form help the cook sort out which ingredients to work with and how to present them. Engaging the creative process results in an artful and satisfactory dish.

Understanding Ingredients and Energetics

To understand an ingredient, whether you have ever seen it before or not, try to place its function and energetic quality in relation to the cooking method. To do this, ask a series of questions that force you to know more about the ingredient. For example, how old is this bean? Has it been on the shelf for two years (in which case I might want to give it back to the earth)? Is it a long-, short-, or medium-cooking bean? What color will it be when it is cooked? Do I need an accent liquid or a major cooking liquid? Will it be too strong in this group of ingredients? Will the salt seasoning change the color drastically? What taste predominates? What role do salt and oil play in this cooking method?

Having a sense of the energetic quality of your ingredients and cooking methods aligns you with their character, their potential, and the seasons. In natural food cookery we determine value from a concept of energy. How much value a food has is reflected in several ways: the vibrancy of the color, the strength of the flesh or seed, the quality of life force that surrounded its growth, and an alive or dead quality. Become sensitive to the energetic quality of cooking methods. How much fire (cooking) will it take to transform the ingredient properly? Do I want to add more fire to the food (cook it longer) because it is cold outside? For example, the marinate method may be a more appropriate way to serve beans in warm weather because this "salad" style of dish requires no extra fire once the beans are cooked; energetically it is cooling. In colder seasons, a long-cooked bean stew with root vegetables may be more appealing.

To consider the energetic value of beans, be aware of the variables that affect texture, including the age of the beans, climate, and altitude. The best beans are eaten within four months of harvesting. A bean loses about ½ percent of its weight per month of storage, all of it lost moisture. When a bean is older than twelve months it has gotten deeper and deeper in dryness. The climate of the bean's birth-place affects how dry a bean may be, which determines the length of time and amount of cooking liquid it will take to rehydrate. Altitude also affects how much time and water a bean requires to cook properly; sea level holds the moisture in beans where high altitudes tend to dry them out. Depending on the cooking method, beans may need about ½ hour longer and anywhere from ½ to 2 cups more liquid per 2,000 feet above sea level (see the Bean Chart on page 45).

Color

Beans offer an array of glorious colors from which to consider an artistic design for a dish or a meal: from white, black, and various shades of brown to deep purple, soft red, yellow, green, and orange. Just because they look one color before you cook them doesn't mean they will hold their color after they are cooked. As you become familiar with the varieties of beans, you will know what color to expect. Or you can refer to the ingredients section of this book.

The color of the beans can be a focal point for the design of the dish or the meal; for example, serve black beans as soup with yellow corn bread and a green and red salad. When the color of the beans is not appealing, find vegetables to enhance the dish (see the Decorative Vegetables Chart on page 10). Even a small quantity of a decorative vegetable can add important color, texture, and taste. Other foods can be used in this role; a few grains sprinkled into a bean salad or soup, for example, function as decorative "vegetables."

Texture

Texture is extremely important in bean cookery. A perfectly cooked bean maintains its integrity, with velvet-smooth, unbroken skin surrounding the soft, luscious meat. Texture is mostly determined in first-stage cooking (the basic cooking that makes the beans edible; see page 16).

In order to cook beans to perfection, you need to count on your cookware and the water ratio. How long you cook the beans in the first stage is not as important as how much liquid you use. Too much liquid will "blast" the beans open, bursting their skins; too little liquid will keep them from getting thoroughly cooked. But too much fire or time does not make a bean "overcooked." In fact, I don't think it is possible to overcook beans.

As important as texture is to bean cookery, it's difficult to ruin this natural food. If the texture isn't right for one dish, it can easily work in another. If your beans have lost their skins, they will still make a good soup. The only texture to avoid at all costs is beans that are too firm, slightly chewy, or, even worse, crunchy—all of which indicate undercooked (indigestible) beans.

Taste and Smell

Did you ever consider training your nose and taste buds to serve you? As servants of your animal passion and instincts, they react without logic. Cooking without them is a handicap because they answer the question of which ingredients go together. If they are not part of your cooking experience, you can train them to become loyal, trustworthy associates. Some people rely more on one than the other, but if you can get them to work together, the effect of their response is undeniable. With their direct links into right-brain memory, we can trust that choices from these senses will not be harmful.

Smell is one of the most powerful receptors we have. It precedes taste to stimulate appetite, but when cooks use the creative process to invent a dish and they command taste and smell to work together, instincts surge into immediate like or dislike.

The human mouth houses response centers for five tastes: sweet at the tip of the tongue, salty at the front sides of the tongue, sour at the side back of the tongue, bitter at the center back of the tongue, and pungent on the walls of the mouth. To receive the fullness of taste that natural foods offer, roll each bite into all the areas as you chew. It is usually obvious when ingredients represent one taste or another. For example, refried beans are sweet since beans are sweet in character, and onions and natural sweetener usually enhance that sweetness in this dish. To round out the balance of tastes in this meal, add some hot salsa and lemon or lime juice in a condiment such as guacamole, and serve with some salty chips to bring pungent, sour, and salty tastes into the meal. To complete the five tastes, add parsley or cilantro to include the bitter flavor. For variation, marinated quinoa would bring sour and bitter into the meal, and a chili sauce would balance the sweet beans with pungent and salty tastes.

The following chart outlines a few ingredients according to taste. When testing ingredients for their taste category, place them in the location of your mouth where the taste buds represent the flavor you suspect. See if they respond more clearly in that part of your mouth.

Our personalities emerge as we season foods with salt seasonings, herbs, spices, oils, and accent liquids. One taste will balance another. Improvise a dish by choosing ingredients represented by the five flavors. Not all five need to appear in every dish; look for balance within the meal as a whole.

TASTE CHART

	SWEET	SOUR	BITTER	PUNGENT	SALTY
GRAINS					
Quinoa			X		
Oats	X				
Rice	X				
BEANS					
Garbanzo	X				
Lentil	X				
Pinto	X				
Navy	X				
COOKING LIQUIDS					
Juice	X	X			
Nut milk	X				
Wine	X	X			
Beer	X		X		
Mirin	X				
Vinegars		X			
SALT SEASONINGS					
Sea salt					X
Tamari/shoyu					X
Umeboshi		X			X
Miso	X				X

Seasoning

Beans love to be seasoned. They have a great capacity to receive a huge variety of flavors. In my mind, the artist makes a careful selection of seasonings, each having a purpose. Haphazardly throwing in this or that is not only wasteful but chaotic, even though it sometimes tastes good. Aim to keep a dish to a minimum number of ingredients, each having a maximum flavor. If the taste is not strong enough, add more of the ingredients you have chosen to create flavor. Sometimes the dish may require another flavor, but usually the right taste can be accomplished by increasing the quantity of one or another.

Seasoning beans usually takes place in second-stage methods (see page 16). Beans are not as bland as grains, but they are denser. A touch of accent liquid, such as vinegar or lime juice, can assist in cutting through the solidness of a bean.

SEASONING WITHOUT MEASURING

When you replace a measuring tool with your fingertips, you feel and see your way through cooking. This crucial act sends messages through the nerves at the end of your fingertips. With their extra-sensitive information bank and a connection to your heart, you are guided to the perfect amount of seasonings to use. This activity strengthens the intuitive nature of your being. As you begin to trust yourself, you strengthen your judgment.

Guidelines for this kind of cooking insure your success. First, determine how many layers of total ingredients lie in the pot or bowl. Imagine what one not-too-thick layer of food would look like smashed and spread across the bottom of your container. Then count upward judging the remaining ingredients to get a total number of layers based on the size of the first layer (see illustration). Second, gather the seasoning in your hand. Move it across the surface of the bowl or pot, dropping some of the ingredients in your hand as if you are brushing the top of each layer with your seasoning. Cross the pot in this fashion for as many times as you have determined there are layers of food. The expression "heavy-handed" comes from just how much of an ingredient a hand releases. So, if the ingredients demand caution, let only a little flow through, or if it is an ingredient that you want to stand out, let more ease through your fingers. Your personality will shine through any dish which you season without measuring. I think this is an incredibly important step for a successful dish.

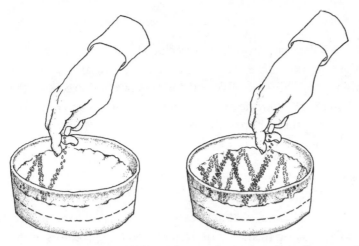

The recipes sometimes call for salt or other seasonings "to taste." This doesn't necessarily mean that you taste the food at that point; rather, it refers you to your intuition to know how much to use. In my classes, I frequently use the term *season to fit,* which to me more clearly explains this process.

Improvisation

Like all art forms that offer improvisation (music, dance, fine arts), it helps to have some additional structure to support your creativity. Use the worksheet in the back of this book to support your composition process, selecting from each category of ingredients: a kind of bean, an oil, a salt seasoning, herbs and spices, a cooking liquid, and sometimes major or decorative vegetables. For most dishes, you will be making a selection from each category. Beginning with one ingredient that either inspires you or fits your dietary limitation, find a companion for it by the taste and smell test. This is an opportunity for your intuitive senses to have an influence on the dish. Taste the ingredients you have chosen to use while you smell one or more ingredients from the category in question. Instantly your body and your being will react with a yes or no, or sometimes, "Well, it doesn't really hit me either way." The last response means that your choice will work. It won't be awful. It might even be really good as you add other ingredients in the same manner.

My rules for improvisation are simple. Don't duplicate in one category unless there is a very good reason (you run out of one and need more but don't want to run to the store is a good enough reason). In other words, don't use olive oil and sesame oil together; but you may bend the rules a bit to include a garnish of olives or sesame seeds when using the opposite oil for its function.

When you truly haven't a clue about which ingredient to use, set the ingredients before you. Just stare at the dish as it is and let your mind stop thinking. Take the fullness of the ingredients that you have chosen into your heart. You may want to close your eyes and when you open them, hopefully not after the dinner guests arrive, your hand will find the perfect ingredient.

Form

Often it is "form" that defines a bean dish, and form is directly related to the cooking method. For example, boiling produces soup, marinating creates a salad, and deep-frying requires a molded shape like a patty or croquette. Where most cookbooks categorize dishes by form, *Romancing the Bean* directs your attention to the cooking method, which in turn determines the form of the dish.

Procedure in Working With the Process

It is difficult to ruin a natural food when you engage the creative process.

The flow of creating a bean dish moves from preliminary treatments to first-stage cooking methods to second-stage cooking methods. *Pretreatments* (soaking and parboiling) prepare the beans to release gassy foam. They are especially important when cooking for tender digestive systems. They are always followed by a *first-stage cooking method* (steeping, pressure-cooking, crock cooking, deep-frying, or sprouting), in which the beans are cooked at length with the intention of making them soft and breaking down the secondary compounds (see page 6). *Second-stage cooking methods* (baking, marinating, refrying, slow cooking, and boiling) turn the beans into a finished dish with your choice of ingredients, form, and flavors. Sprouting and marinating are not technically cooking methods, but they function as first-stage and second-stage methods without heat.

First, determine whether the bean is a short-, medium-, or long-cooking bean and bring it through a first-stage cooking method. Then take a good look at the texture of the bean to determine which second-stage method would be best for the form you need. Using taste and smell with sensitivity to color, select ingredients from the major categories (oil, salt seasoning, cooking liquid, herbs and spices, and vegetables).

Serving Beans in a Meal

Beans can be daily fare for breakfast, lunch, or dinner, or they can appear in just about any course in a formal meal. As an appetizer, beans could be a pâté, spread, or dip. Soup could be a multi vegetable and bean soup, or a single kind of bean partially pureed. Salad possibilities include marinated beans, with or without other vegetables. Beans can accompany a main dish grain as a sauce or as a side dish, such as beans steeped with root vegetables or beans baked in sauce. I have been known to make bean brownies, but that is a stretch.

A good ratio of beans to grain is about 1:4. In other words, don't eat too many. For all their lusciousness, too many beans can be uncomfortable even if they are cooked thoroughly. For a side dish of beans allow about ¼ to ½ cup of cooked beans per serving.

Ingredients

To know an ingredient is to know how to cook it. In this chapter ingredients are classified into categories that are defined by function. When you witness how they function, you will be able to use a variety of ingredients within that category.

Beans

All beans hold an innate strength and power. But each has a quality distinguishing it and determining how appropriate it may be for certain cooking methods. In the following pages, I have characterized each bean according to its cooking time (long, medium, or short); my subjective impression of its energetic qualities; the color of beans after they have been cooked; some favorite cooking methods; a nutritional profile in grams per 100-gram serving; and the yield (how much volume you get from one cup of dry beans when they are cooked).

Understanding ingredients propels you into chefdom. When we look at food, we see a character. It has a quality, a feel, a sense to it. Sometimes looking at a food simply tells us if it is dead or alive.

ANASAZI
Medium-cooking bean

This ancient Anasazi Indian staple could be the granddaddy of pinto beans. Raw, you can clearly see the gorgeous purple splotchy design against the white background, mimicking pinto horses and grand canyons of nature. This interesting pattern dissolves into the pot, leaving the cooked beans a soft pinkish tan color. Not too big, about ½ inch in length when cooked, Anasazi beans are a favorite for chili and refried beans. You might also find Bolita beans, another ancient strain related to the modern pinto. It's one of the most sensual of beans, gorgeous and voluptuous in taste and texture.

ENERGETICS:
Quiet, contained, powerfully seductive
COLOR:
Soft brownish-mauve
FAVORITE COOKING METHODS:
Boil, sauce, refry
NUTRITIONAL PROFILE:
23g protein, 64g carbohydrates, 1.5g fat, 6mg sodium
YIELD:
1 cup dry = 2½ cups cooked

AZUKI
Medium- to short-cooking bean

There are several ways to pronounce the name of this bean. I say aduki. Some people speak the "s" or "z" (adsuki or adzuki), giving the tongue more to do. Others leave the "d" out all together and sing it high on the scale — azuki or asuki. It's an unusual tasting bean. Accommodating salty and sweet flavors, it has a slightly sharp, bitter aftertaste. That must be why it loves to be sweetened. Traditional Japanese cooking gives this bean a respectful position in desserts and ceremonial dishes. Azuki beans hold their color during and after cooking. This is one of my favorite beans for cooking with rice (especially sweet rice); the beans strongly influence the color of the rice, leaving it a beautiful mauve-

ENERGETICS:
Starchy, deep-tasting, small but carries a big stick
COLOR:
Purple
FAVORITE COOKING METHODS:
Slow cook
NUTRITIONAL PROFILE:
13g protein, 35g carbohydrates, 1g fat, 5mg sodium
YIELD:
1 cup dry = 3 cups cooked

brown. A good quality azuki bean is deep purple-brown, shiny, small (about ¼ inch long), and has a thin white smile in the seam of its coat.

BLACK TURTLE
Medium-cooking bean

Black beans originated in South America, acquiring names such as Mexican black beans and Spanish black beans. I like the name black turtle, not because they remind me of turtles, but because in American Indian lore, the continent of the Americas was referred to as Turtle Island. When cooked, they shine. Black turtle beans hold their shape and individuality quite well, making them versatile and good for all cooking methods.

BLACK-EYED PEA
Short- to medium-cooking bean

This tropical Old World pea-that's-a-bean was brought into the South with the slave trade. The pattern of black and white in a group of these beans looks like a society in action, a group of individuals in relationship. Also known as cowpeas, southern beans, or cream peas, this versatile food is best known in Southern cooking. Although it is often cooked with bacon or ham, it radiates a powerful sweet, delicious taste all by itself.

CANNELLINI
Medium-cooking bean

This variation of the white bean group is a cousin to navy and great northern beans. It's a little longer and fatter than the great northern, but they act and taste alike. In a white bean salad, cannellini beans will be more present and voluptuous than the smaller types. They hold their shape well.

ENERGETICS:
Modest, delicate, full nutty flavor
COLOR:
Deep black-purple
FAVORITE COOKING METHODS:
Boil, marinate, sauce
NUTRITIONAL PROFILE:
22g protein, 61g carbohydrates, 1.5g fat, 8mg sodium
YIELD:
1 cup dry = 2½ cups cooked

ENERGETICS:
Soft, delicate, ultra-smooth
COLOR:
Pale rosy
FAVORITE COOKING METHODS:
Slow cook, pâté
NUTRITIONAL PROFILE:
23g protein, 62g carbohydrate, 1.5g fat, 35mg sodium
YIELD:
1 cup dry = 2½ cups cooked

ENERGETICS:
Elegant, long
COLOR:
Off-white to tan
FLAVOR:
Sweet and earthy
FAVORITE COOKING METHODS:
Boil, marinate
NUTRITIONAL PROFILE:
22g protein, 61g carbohydrates, 1.5g fat, 8mg sodium
YIELD:
1 cup dry = 3 cups cooked

CHICK-PEA or GARBANZO

Long-cooking bean

The chick-pea, one of the most famous beans in history, dates back to at least 5000 B.C. in the Mediterranean region. Its Latin name, *Cicer arietinum,* attests to its high regard in ancient Rome; the great leader Cicero took his family name from the chick-pea, and the other name comes from the word for ram, the firmness and shape of the bean being like that of the two-horned animal.

The Spanish name garbanzo is derived from Greek, and in Greece and other Mediterranean countries this bean is used in marinades, soups, falafel, and dips and spreads. In India, the chick-pea is the country's most important legume. It covers almost as much acreage as wheat.

Extra firm and spherical in shape, the dry garbanzo bean looks like a well-traveled globe or a replica of the human brain. Measuring only ¼ inch, this small dry bean swells to at least twice its size during the required soaking period, after which it is ready for all cooking methods including deep-frying. It's hard to believe that this gnarly, pea-shaped bean transforms itself into the richest, most luscious of all beans. When perfectly cooked, the chick-pea maintains its sphere, but the surface is smooth and the plump, rich meat is held gracefully within a thin membrane.

This is also the fattiest bean. Now don't panic over the word fat. Nature has placed a generous amount of fat in chick-peas, but it's in balance with the other nutrients, so we can enjoy a smooth luscious chestnut flavor and rich experience.

Legends of the Middle East say that plants of the black kabouli variety attract thunderstorms during their flowering stage. These black chick-peas are small, gemlike, steel-colored nuggets that at first sight could be mistaken for genuine rocks.

ENERGETICS:
Sweet, strong, deep, rich, multifaceted
COLOR:
Buff
FAVORITE COOKING METHODS:
Bake, spread, marinate
NUTRITIONAL PROFILE:
20g protein, 61g carbohydrates, 5g fat, 7mg sodium
YIELD:
1 dry cup = 2½ cups cooked

CRANBERRY

Medium-cooking bean

This is a good example of how farmers create and proliferate beans. Similar to pinto beans, cranberry beans have a richer, more interesting color and design pattern on the outside; but when cooked, they are rather dull. They are increasingly available as fresh shelling beans, and you might want to experiment with them in this form.

ENERGETICS:
Mellow, attractive
COLOR:
Cranberry pink
FAVORITE COOKING METHODS:
Slow cook (pâté)
NUTRITIONAL PROFILE:
23g protein, 64g carbohydrates, 1g fat, 6mg sodium
YIELD:
1 cup dry = 2½ cups cooked

ENERGETICS:
Stubborn, tough, and meaty
COLOR:
Light brown
FLAVOR:
Sweet with a medicinal af-
tertaste
FAVORITE COOKING
METHODS:
None
NUTRITIONAL PROFILE:
28g protein, 58g carbohy-
drates, 2g fat
YIELD:
1 cup dry = 2 cups cooked

ENERGETICS:
Average, almost invisible
COLOR:
Off-white
FAVORITE COOKING
METHODS:
Boil, bake
NUTRITIONAL PROFILE:
22g protein, 61g carbohy-
drates, 2g fat, 19mg sodium
YIELD:
1 cup dry = 2½ cups cooked

ENERGETICS:
Enticing, luring, luscious
COLOR:
Deep red
FAVORITE COOKING
METHODS:
Marinate, sauce, boil, refry,
bake
NUTRITIONAL PROFILE:
22g protein, 62g carbohy-
drates, 1.5g fat, 7mg sodium
YIELD:
1 cup dry = 3 cups cooked.

FAVA
Long-cooking bean

This ancient Egyptian bean is also called broad bean, Windsor, or horse bean. Fava beans are huge. I can just imagine the Roman leader Fabius eating them. (His family name actually came from this bean, attesting to its importance in the ancient Mediterranean world.) I prefer the name horse beans, which reflects their tough skins and sweet taste similar to that of the season's very first green pea. But trying to find a good second-stage cooking method for them was difficult. They do not yield to a smooth texture very easily. I suspect that throughout history this bean was ground to meal or flour and used in gruel, baked goods, and falafel-style dishes. They require a good long soak, and I found in cooking them that they were uneven, some being thoroughly cooked while others remained hard. Progresso brand has an acceptable version in cans.

GREAT NORTHERN
Medium-cooking bean

These are the full-grown, dried seeds of the common green bean. Great northern beans were the most widely used bean in America. Stemming from a traditional Boston baked bean dish, a Saturday night ritual, and integrating the French dish *cassoulet,* these beans managed to become famous despite the reliance on meat in this dish. I like the size of this bean; it's not too big, not too small. No dominant flavors stand out, so its compatibility with other beans makes a good soup. Pureed it makes a good cream-style base for soup and sauces.

KIDNEY
Medium-cooking bean

This is a very popular bean. It's classy. Americans recognize it in the famous Three Bean Salad (see recipe, page 108). I have noticed a great difference between the organic and commercial varieties in this bean. It seems the skins will stay intact better if they are organically grown, whereas the commercial bean's skin easily detaches. Organically grown beans also yield a deeper, more distinct taste.

LENTIL, GREEN
Short-cooking bean

Like little specks of earth, lentils are an ancient and renowned food. One of the oldest beans known, this seed was available to early gathering cultures and was the first of the Old World beans to be domesticated. Its Latin name and double convex shape gave us the word *lens* for a similarly shaped piece of optical glass.

I prefer the green French variety, which is smaller and deeper in color and taste than the common brown lentil. It also holds its shape more clearly.

ENERGETICS:
Dainty, soft
COLOR:
Light to dark green
FAVORITE COOKING METHODS:
Bake (pâté), marinate, boil
NUTRITIONAL PROFILE:
25g protein, 60g carbohydrates, 1g fat, 7mg sodium
YIELD:
1 cup dry = 3 cups cooked

LENTIL, RED
Short-cooking bean

Softer than green lentils, red lentils act more like a split pea than a bean. They start out with a beautiful peachy color and end up an iridescent light yellow/pea green. The reproductive section of a red lentil, a moon-shaped sliver, accents the dish. I like these beans best as soup. At high altitude they replace the difficult-to-cook split pea but give the same full-tasting, silky weight as a good split pea. These are short-cooking beans; they do not require soaking. Do not pressure-cook them; they cook so quickly that pressure-cooking is unnecessary, and with no skin to contain the meat, it "explodes" into the liquid and could clog the valve.

ENERGETICS:
Light, dreamy, enchanting
COLOR:
Yellow-green
FAVORITE COOKING METHODS:
Boil
NUTRITIONAL PROFILE:
25g protein, 62g carbohydrate 1g fat, 7mg sodium
YIELD:
1 cup dry = 4 cups cooked

LIMA
Short- to medium-cooking bean

I am one of those people who could live without lima beans. I love their shape, but they have a tricky personality. Even though they appear to be delicate and deeply flavored, they are extremely gassy for my body. But they really love to be cooked in interesting ways.

ENERGETICS:
Universal
COLOR:
Off-white tannish green
FAVORITE COOKING METHODS:
Boil, slow cook, refry
NUTRITIONAL PROFILE:
20g protein, 64g carbohydrates, 2g fat, 9mg sodium
YIELD:
1 cup dry = 2½ cups cooked

ENERGETICS:
Ready to burst
COLOR:
Greenish brown; translucent
white when sprouted
FAVORITE COOKING
METHODS:
Sprouts, refried, marinated
NUTRITIONAL PROFILE:
4g protein, 7g carbohydrates,
0g fat, 4mg sodium
YIELD: 1 cup dry=4 cups
sprouted

MUNG
Short-cooking bean

Similar to azuki beans in looks and cooked texture, this bean has two lives. It's known primarily as sprouts, in which the head disappears into a three-inch tail. I love this transformation. Mung bean sprouts are by far the easiest beans to eat. I have tried the Indian recipes for mung bean pancakes, but found them difficult to digest. Mung beans may be cooked in soup or slow-cooked dishes, but they require many spices to accommodate their power.

ENERGETICS:
Intense, buttonlike
COLOR:
Off-white to tan
FAVORITE COOKING
METHODS:
Boil, bake
NUTRITIONAL PROFILE:
22g protein, 61g carbohy-
drates, 2g fat, 19mg sodium
YIELD:
1 cup dry=3 cups cooked

NAVY
Medium-cooking bean

Relative to cannellini and great northern beans, navy beans are the smallest in the family. Brought to Boston through the Navy, this bean is one of the *flageolets,* a group of white beans from Europe. The name makes me think of a seductive chorus line of beautiful beans.

ENERGETICS:
Smooth, fat, satisfying
COLOR:
Tannish pink
FAVORITE COOKING
METHODS:
Boil, refry.
NUTRITIONAL PROFILE:
23g protein, 64g carbohy-
drates, 1g fat, 10mg sodium
YIELD:
1 cup dry=3 cups cooked

PINTO
Medium-cooking bean

Pinto beans are a hybrid from a very strong heirloom variety of Mexican beans. They become plump, meaty, luscious morsels ready for just about anything. Given their Mexican origin, pinto beans love to be cooked with chilies, epazote, lime, and beer.

SMALL RED

Medium-cooking bean

Similar to black turtle beans only red, this bean has all the versatility of the black bean. It is great for color, taste, and texture in all cooking methods. The small red bean is especially good to use when you don't want a large kidney bean.

ENERGETICS:
Stocky
COLOR:
Deep red
FAVORITE COOKING METHODS:
Boil, bake, refry
NUTRITIONAL PROFILE:
23g protein, 64g carbohydrates, 1g fat, 5mg sodium
YIELD:
1 cup dry = 2½ cups cooked

SOYBEAN

Long-cooking bean

Names for this bean reach outside its sound into majestic realms where one can feel the importance of this food. Names like "miracle bean," "meat of the soil," and "the cow of China" indicate the power of this simple food. You don't purchase soybeans in a standard grocery the way you would purchase pinto, kidney, or black beans. You can't even get them cooked whole in a can. So why are soybeans the largest, single most important seed crop in the economy of this great country? The wealth of this magnificent seed comes in the many ways its power is transformed. Plants are used as green manure to rebuild the soil and to provide forage for animals. Fresh beans are eaten as a vegetable, processed into cooking oil and lecithin and also into nonfood products, such as glycerin, enamels, varnish, waterproof goods, linoleum, paints, soap, celluloid, rubber substitute, printing ink, lighting, lubrication, and candles. Whole, dry beans used primarily as animal feed also respond to the cooking methods for human consumption described in *Romancing the Bean*. Processed soybeans parade as coffee substitute, soy milk, bean curd and fermented cake (tofu and tempeh—see page 127), soysage (fiber with sausage flavorings), soy sauce (tamari), miso, and texturized vegetable protein (TVP), which becomes filler for many prepared food products.

(For some reason, vegetable protein has always been judged in the shadow of meat and meat products. Yet soybeans are used to boost the protein value of meat products in such products as deli turkey and ham. The nutritional battle is endless and really goes nowhere. Look instead at the energetic quality of a food. Do you want to eat the energy of a cow or a fish or a plant?)

ENERGETICS:
Humble, tight little seeds holding dormant possibilities of changing the world; strong, complex flavors
COLOR:
Yellowish-tan or purple-black
FAVORITE COOKING METHODS:
Yellow – sprouted, refry
Black – slow cook, boil
NUTRITIONAL PROFILE:
34g protein, 26g carbohydrates, 17.5g fat; phosphorus, calcium, iron
YIELD:
1 cup dry = 3 cups cooked

Even though the soybean was honored at tables of vegetarian Buddhists in early China, where it originated, it wasn't until the seventeenth century that the West was introduced to this magnificent source of protein and oil. Upon introduction, the West proceeded to manufacture paint, soap, and varnishes with soybeans, overlooking their dietary value for humankind.

The yellow soybean, small, round, unfolding to about ½ an inch in length when soaked, has a silky texture when cooked. Black soybeans, as tales are told, sweeten a singer's voice. With somewhat fatter spheres than the yellow soybean, the black soybean cooks to a larger seed. To cook these so that the skin is intact and the center is soft takes a careful watch and attention to the water ratio. Black soybeans are extremely sweet and nutty, but it is not appropriate to pressure-cook them. Long soaking and crock cooking are best.

SPLIT PEA
Short-cooking bean

Whether green or yellow, these brilliantly represent peas. Whole dry peas are incredibly stubborn about becoming soft, and I gave up trying to cook them twenty years ago. But the split pea has rescued the family name. Split peas, being split, do not maintain their shape; like red lentils, they become thick and pastelike. If they don't lose their shape, they are usually not cooked.

TONGUE OF FIRE
Long-cooking bean

These big, voluptuous, perfectly shaped beans deserve to be pricey. When served whole, they inspire unusual responses. It seems a shame to blend them, for their beauty lies in the grand tiger stripes across the girth. Unlike other beans that lose their stripes when cooked, tongue of fire beans show a deep colored purple stripe beneath the lighter purple coating. Little is known of this fashionable bean. I suspect it has come from Europe with other exotic bean varieties.

ENERGETICS:
Formless, mutable
COLOR:
Yellow or green
FAVORITE COOKING METHODS:
Boil, refry
NUTRITIONAL PROFILE:
24g protein, 63g carbohydrates, 1g fat, 40mg sodium
YIELD:
1 cup dry = 5 cups cooked

ENERGETICS:
Smoky, fat and sassy
COLOR:
Purple
FAVORITE COOKING METHODS:
Marinate
NUTRITIONAL PROFILE:
Unknown; probably compares to other dry beans

Salt Seasonings

The purpose of salt is to bring the character of ingredients into harmony. Salt commands the ingredients to open their cell structure, releasing their flavors to mingle and merge in the dish.

In this style of cooking, there are five kinds of salt seasonings: plain sea salt, vegetable salt, miso, tamari, and umeboshi vinegar. Although sea salt is compatible with all the other salts, it can stand alone as the salt seasoning. I strongly recommend that you do not combine any of the other salt seasonings. Each has a distinct contribution to the dish. To use more than one would be redundant in function and confusing to taste.

SEA SALT

In bean cookery, sea salt brings about the sweetness and full flavor of beans. Some people think salt helps the digestibility of beans. Honest salt (dehydrated seawater) is never applied to food directly. It must be dissolved by the cooking liquid to become more usable for the body. It usually takes about 10 minutes to integrate the function of salt when heated. In cold dishes, you should beat the salt for several minutes to have it function fully.

I feel dramatically involved with this ingredient. It is probably the most important element in cooking, for it is solely responsible for the success of a dish. Without it, food not only isn't available to the body, but it leaves a major hole in the eating experience so that eventually the body develops cravings. Salt is not used to create a salty taste. Most of the plant world is extremely sweet when properly transformed. Salt is the transformer.

According to salt scholar Jacques de Langre, the quality of salt you choose to use will either assist the power of natural foods in the body or interfere with the food's potential nutrition. "When a person fails to respond and get well on a natural diet of whole grains and vegetables, the failure can usually be traced directly to the use of falsely labeled natural salt, boiled or refined salt, or to a total lack of salt. The total absence of any salt greatly inhibits absorption of grains and vegetables and renders them unable to function as 'medicine.'" He says that physicians in European medical circles "invariably prescribe a return to the use of mineral-rich natural sea salt and obtain total remission in a multitude of diseases."

REMEMBER: All salts should be kept out of first-stage cooking methods.

ENERGETICS:
Crystalline in purity, holding the richness of the sea
COLOR:
Off-white to pure white
TASTE:
Salty (two to four times the strength of table salt)
COOKING METHODS:
All second-stage methods
NUTRITIONAL PROFILE:
Sodium and trace minerals not found in earth plants

Many of the same ingredients and seasonings used in bean cookery are also used in cooking grain. Refer to Amazing Grains *for a deeper perspective on these ingredients.*

To check the quality of the salt you are using, examine where it comes from. Some of the best sea salt is harvested through flowing channels over clay beds. The water is dried by the energy of the wind and sun. Skilled workers rake the salt without accumulating clay in the finished product. Other salt is harvested in cement beds where the water is static or from earthy deposits where there was once a body of saltwater. Free-flowing table salt also contains chemical agents, dextrose, cornstarch, and usually iodine. Although only a trace of iodine is needed in the body, it becomes an additive to table salt because unlike true sea salt, which contains this trace mineral along with approximately 80 others, table salt lacks these components in a natural, balanced relationship.

You might question what difference does it make as long as we get the iodine? Energetics, that is the difference. A quality natural product has little interference from the time it leaves the earth and reaches our plate. Processing and overhandling alter the energetic quality of an ingredient. Consider the complicated process and the additional components given to table salt to make the color, flow, and addictive taste.

You cannot put sea salt directly on the food; its energetic quality is too pure and powerful. But table salt, diluted and polluted, simply pours onto your food. And that is just what American people have done—hence the overuse and fear of salt. Actually, it is not salt itself we should fear; it is the misuse of poor quality salt that has created the problems. Good quality sea salt is energetically pure, crystalline. It moved naturally from the sea, over the earth, with no additives, no chemical alterations.

This salt will feel anywhere from moist and soft to dry and hard. This doesn't matter. However, you must use your fingertips to judge how much to use because it is much saltier than other salts.

VEGETABLE SALT

With a combination of dehydrated vegetables, herbs, and spices, this ingredient performs two functions. It provides the basic flavor of sea salt, plus additional flavors such as one would find in a prepared mix of soup stock or other custom seasonings. Two of my favorites are Spike and Old Bay. The first ingredient on the label of these salt seasonings is salt (the first ingredient in a label means that that ingredient is the largest quantity and the following ingredients represent smaller amounts in descending order).

ENERGETICS:
Complicated and potent
COLOR:
Varies; usually from golden brown to red
FLAVOR:
Salty; varies from aromatic to pungent
COOKING METHODS:
All second-stage methods
NUTRITIONAL PROFILE:
Minerals

The following salt seasonings are combinations of food, water, salt, and time, which is a way of processing straight salt not only to create delicious seasonings, but to make the sodium element kinder and more available to the body. Salt seasonings have extra power, not just seasoning power. Beneficial enzymes are part of their essence.

MISO

This salt seasoning is used most discreetly in bean cookery, because to me it is redundant. Miso is a bean itself, a fermented paste of soybeans, *koji* rice, salt, and water. It is a traditional food from Japan. The varieties of miso range from dark to light, salty to sweet; usually, the darker the miso, the saltier it will be. Dark miso can color your bean dish, deepening its natural shade. This is particularly noticeable in the lentil pâté dish on page 65.

The most common way to use miso in bean cookery is blended into a spread or diluted in bean juice or other cooking liquid for a sauce. However, don't boil miso if you want the beneficial enzymes it offers.

I strongly suggest storing miso in the refrigerator, even though you don't have to. As it rests at room temperature (68 degrees F or higher), it continues to ferment, occasionally revealing white spots of friendly bacteria. There's no need to throw out this miso; just remove the white spots. A form of miso is also made from the chick-pea (garbanzo bean). Chickpeaso is extremely sweet and quite compatible with garbanzo bean dishes. But it is not as salty as a darker miso, so be prepared to use it in combination with sea salt. Chickpeaso is particularly delicious to people who are sensitive to soy products.

ENERGETICS:
Like moist earth
COLOR:
Varies from creamy white to buff to golden to brown to almost black
FLAVOR:
Rich, sweet to salty, fermented like wine
COOKING METHODS:
Hot and cold sauces, soup, pâté, spreads
NUTRITIONAL PROFILE:
13 to 20% protein, 12% sodium, B vitamins including B12

TAMARI, SHOYU

These delicious seasonings are naturally brewed, like fine wine. They have subtle aftertaste flavors while the base taste is salty. Soy sauce, the common name for this kind of seasoning, sometimes is prepared with caramel coloring and all sorts of ingredients except salt. So, if your soy sauce is not a naturally brewed one, check to see if there is any salt present at all. Without real salt, the ingredient won't perform. Tamari is brewed with soybeans, salt, water, and rice. Shoyu also includes wheat or wheat flour.

In bean cookery, tamari or shoyu acts to complete the flavoring of a dish. Refried beans, bean soup, dipping sauce for croquettes, and braising liquids are favorite places for this salt seasoning. It does not need to be refrigerated.

ENERGETICS:
Clear and clean, like liquid onyx
COLOR:
Auburn-black
FLAVOR:
Salty, fermented
COOKING METHODS:
Boil, refry, slow cook, bake
NUTRITIONAL PROFILE:
Trace of protein

ENERGETICS:
Brilliant, vital, charging
COLOR:
Light pink
TASTE:
Salty-sour with fruit overtones
COOKING METHODS:
All second-stage methods
NUTRITIONAL PROFILE:
Sodium and acid

UMEBOSHI VINEGAR

Don't be misled by the title. This ingredient is a salt seasoning first and an accent liquid second. It is complex in taste, being both salty and sour. Salt combined with plums or apricots and a beefsteak (*shiso*) leaf draws out liquid over time and produces a lovely combination of flavors. My favorite use of this ingredient is in spreads and pâtés, but I trust it can go in many other places.

One has to be careful placing sour or acid flavors with beans because they initiate a decomposition of the bean. When this taste is controlled through culinary skill and refrigeration, it is a safe combination. When the sour flavor evolves through time and temperature or saliva, the bean is not safe to eat. Develop a clear tasting tongue. The advantage of umeboshi vinegar is that the salt content acts as a preservative, restricting immediate breakdown of the bean.

Cooking Liquids

Cooking liquid has three functions: (1) to rehydrate beans in the first stage; (2) as a major cooking liquid, to adjust substance in the second stage; (3) as a minor cooking liquid, to accent the taste of a dish.

Major cooking liquids, such as water, stock, and vegetable juice, account for the substance and volume of a dish. They are used in the first stage to help beans swell to their full size and create bean juice. The amount of liquid in the second stage determines the substance (thick or thin) of the dish. Minor cooking liquids, such as vinegars, citrus juice, beer, or wine, lighten the dish or give it a kick, round out the flavors, or draw a distinct taste.

In bean cookery, the cooking liquid for first-stage methods is almost always water. On occasion, using a little sherry, sake, wine, or beer with water or vegetable stock as the primary cooking liquid is appropriate. If you use any liquid other than water, the beans will not keep as long or be as versatile in second-stage methods.

Minor, or accent, liquids help lighten the intensity of a bean dish, which tends to be very concentrated, sometimes giving a heavy feeling. Accent liquids are primarily used with spreads, pâtés, and marinated, baked, and refried bean dishes.

WATER

Major cooking liquid

This ingredient, frequently taken for granted, is essential in bean cookery. Dry beans demand water. Obviously, water rehydrates the beans either in soaking or in first-stage methods. Another way to value water is to notice its clear energy and how it encourages the bean to expand into its full character.

But water is not appropriate in second-stage methods with the exception of soups and sauces (boiling) because it dilutes the character too much. Accent liquids and other substance liquids that offer additional character to a dish and not just reflect what is there, are more appropriate for the majority of second-stage methods.

ENERGETICS:
Clear, clean, neutral, revitalizing
COLOR:
None
FLAVOR:
Only slight variations in flavor
COOKING METHODS:
All first-stage; boiling (soup)
NUTRITIONAL PROFILE:
Essential for life

BEAN JUICE

Major and minor cooking liquid

This cooking liquid is the juice or broth created by the first-stage method. So when preparing beans for soup or salad, there could be bean juice from the first-stage method. Some people save the juice, but it keeps only a few days refrigerated. It can be frozen.

ENERGETICS:
Cloudy, heavy, rich with flavor of the bean
COLOR:
Shades of the bean of your choice
FLAVOR:
Rich to subtle; diluted memories of the bean
COOKING METHODS:
Boil, marinate
NUTRITIONAL PROFILE:
Unknown; presumably reflects that of the bean

RICE MILK

Major cooking liquid

This natural milklike liquid is packaged under the brand name Rice Dream (Imagine Foods, Inc., 299 California Ave., Palo Alto, CA 94306). It is a lovely major cooking liquid that adds a white color to your dish. You could also cook rice in a ratio of 8:1, blend and strain it. It won't be drinkable like Rice Dream, but you could use it as a second-stage cooking liquid.

ENERGETICS:
Angelic, clean feeling
COLOR:
White or off-white
FLAVOR:
Sweet
COOKING METHODS:
Boil, slow cook
NUTRITIONAL PROFILE:
1g protein, 28g carbohydrates, 2g fat, 80mg sodium per cup

ENERGETICS:
Spirit-filled water, mineral
rich, light
COLOR:
Depends on the vegetables;
light green to golden brown
FLAVOR:
Depends on the vegetables
COOKING METHODS:
Pressure-cook, steep, boil,
sauce
NUTRITIONAL PROFILE:
Varies

ENERGETICS:
Exotic, opening up energy
COLOR:
Clear to red
FLAVORS:
Fruity to grainy
COOKING METHODS:
All
NUTRITIONAL PROFILE:
Varies

ENERGETICS:
Rich, luscious, creamy
COLOR:
Off-white
FLAVOR:
Mildly nutty
COOKING METHODS:
Boil, slow cook
NUTRITIONAL PROFILE:
Mostly fat, some protein and
carbohydrate

VEGETABLE STOCK OR BOUILLON

Major cooking liquid

I don't usually go to the effort of making a vegetable stock for bean dishes because there are so many flavors coming forward from the beans, oil, salt seasoning, vegetables, herbs, and spices. But if a vegetable stock is handy, I love to use it in bean soup. The most important place to consider using a vegetable stock is in the clear soups, such as the Clear Soup With Tofu on page 154.

Vegetable bouillon cubes, on the other hand, can be used to embellish soups and sauces quickly. Remember to reduce other salt seasonings when using salted bouillon, and do not use a salted bouillon in first-stage methods. I like Morga brand.

BEER, WINE, SAKE

Major and minor cooking liquids

In small doses, these cooking liquids add dimension to a sauce or bean dish. They work beautifully in first-stage methods when combined with water (see Anasazi Chili, page 98, and Black-Eyed Peas in Rosemary and Lemon, page 71).

NUT MILK

Major and minor cooking liquid

Nut milks are particularly good to create the illusion of dairy products in soups and sauces. Make a thin nut milk for bean dishes, using ¼ cup nuts to 2 cups of liquid. Much more than that will be too rich in protein and the dish could appear heavy. Blend raw nuts in a blender with major cooking liquid until all is smooth. You may want to strain the small nut meats away from the milk, depending on the texture of your dish and how elegant the presentation must be. To make nut milk in a food processor, first blend nuts to a smooth paste. Add water slowly allowing time for the paste to thicken, then add remaining water.

VEGETABLE JUICE

Major cooking liquid

It might require a vegetable juicer for you to take full advantage of the creativity available with vegetable juice as a major cooking liquid. Those of you who have juicers will enjoy combinations of root, stalk, and leaf vegetables, such as carrots, beets, parsnips, celery, Swiss chard, and lettuce as liquid for your bean dishes. Other options may be to purchase this liquid at a health-food store, or consider canned V-8 brand juice from the supermarket. I know that cooking live juice qualifies as a sin in some circles, so make some extra to drink fresh.

ENERGETICS:
Mineral rich, fragrant
COLOR:
Depends on the vegetable; pale green to deep purple
FLAVOR:
Frequently sweet and earthy
COOKING METHODS:
All except pâté and spreads, where no major cooking liquid is required
NUTRITIONAL PROFILE:
High in vitamins and minerals

FRUIT JUICE

Major and minor cooking liquid

I hardly ever consider putting sweet fruit juice with beans as a major cooking liquid. It just seems like a volatile combination. But allowing for "the process," there will no doubt be a dish in which this cooking liquid works beautifully. Consider the sweetness of some apple, pineapple, or cherry juice in a baked bean dish. Lemon, lime, and orange juices are used frequently as minor cooking liquids in marinades, to lighten spreads (see Hot Pepper Hummus, page 120) and to complete soups (see Black Bean Soup, page 100).

ENERGETICS:
Peripheral, far-reaching
COLOR:
Varies with fruit from light and clear to dark red
FLAVOR:
Strong, definitive flavors, either sweet or sour
COOKING METHODS:
Marinades, spreads, sauces, dips, boil
NUTRITIONAL PROFILE:
Carbohydrates, sugar

VINEGAR

Minor cooking liquid

Vinegars are particularly useful in bean cookery to lighten or balance the intensity of the bean. It may only take 1 teaspoon in 5 quarts of soup to shift the energy of the soup. You don't necessarily want the bean to taste sour; you might just want the flavors to dance a little differently.

The large variety of vinegars available offers many opportunities to put that special edge on your bean dish. Apple cider is the most friendly to the body, and vinegars made from rice, wine, and berries also offer lovely flavors. Sometimes these are flavored with herbs and spices. They are great gifts and particularly useful in marinades and basting sauces. Distilled vinegar, as far as I am concerned, is for cleaning drains.

ENERGETICS:
Sharp, cutting, intense
COLOR:
Light and clear to dark and cloudy radish brown
FLAVOR:
Sour; sometimes hints of sweetness
COOKING METHODS:
Spreads, sauces, boil, marinate
NUTRITIONAL PROFILE:
Stimulates digestion

HERBS AND SPICES CHART

This chart indicates origins of herbs and spices. You can use it as a way to begin thinking of combining ingredients that come from the same place. For example, a European dish may have basil or tarragon, a Middle Eastern dish may have cumin and cinnamon. The * symbol indicates dominant herbs, which provide the main taste when combined with other ingredients. The remaining herbs and spices are compatible with each other and with the dominant ingredients.

	EUROPEAN	MIDDLE EASTERN	ORIENTAL	LATIN AMERICAN	INDIAN
Allspice				X	
Basil	X				
Bay leaf	X			X	X
Chervil	X				
Dill	X				
*Caraway	X				
*Cardamom					X
*Cilantro		X	X	X	
*Coriander		X			X
*Cinnamon	X	X	X	X	X
*Cumin	X	X	X	X	X
Fennel	X				
Garam Masala					X
Garlic	X	X	X	X	
Ginger			X		X
*Marjoram	X	X			
*Mint		X	X		
Mustard	X		X		
Nutmeg		X			X
Oregano	X			X	
Parsley	X	X	X	X	X
Pepper	X	X			X
*Rosemary	X				
Saffron		X			X
*Sage	X				
Savory	X				
*Tarragon	X				
Thyme	X				
Turmeric		X			X

Herbs and Spices

Beans invite herbs and spices into them with little discrimination. Some cultures infuse ten or more ingredients into a bean dish. I like to keep it simple, most of the time emphasizing one to three (if you count garlic and shallots). But some dishes demand many herbs and spices, such as Anasazi Chili (page 98) or Savory Tofu Pie (page 148).

When selecting from this ingredient category, consult your taste and smell senses. If you don't trust that process yet (described on page 15), use the chart on page 34 listing ethnic groupings of herbs and spices. Frequently I cross over the borders and mix and match for unusual experiences. But then relying on the taste and smell test is essential. Some examples of unusual combinations of flavors are the Black Bean and Rice Croquettes on page 84, where orange flower water meets garam masala and garlic, or White Bean Soup (page 94), with garlic, pickling spices, crushed red pepper, and natural hickory smoke flavoring.

Vegetables

Vegetables in bean cookery can have a major or minor position. The onion family holds an everpresent position. Any member can take part in any bean dish; white, yellow, purple, and green onions along with shallots or garlic can be used interchangeably in most dishes. Avoid the cabbage family when cooking beans. I find that they fight for which can produce the most gas, and together they can be unbearable. White, green, and purple cabbages and brussels sprouts are tempting to use for their delicious taste and color, but don't.

Oil

Oil helps to smooth out the texture of a bean dish as it carries flavors from herbs, spices, and vegetables to deepen the taste. Most often, you can use as little or as much as you like without hurting the success of the dish. But there may be some concern about the quantity even with exceptional quality.

Purchase the purest, highest quality of oil you can. I recommend expeller pressed oils. You can usually identify them by their full taste, representing the foods from which they were made. In this system of cookery, we use very few ingredients. Each one has to count, contributing flavor and character whenever appropriate. Lighter oils are best suited for dry beans, and heavier oils, such as dark sesame, are more suitable for tofu and tempeh, the lighter beans.

Oil comes in several forms and flavors. Here are some guidelines to help you. But please know that oils are interchangeable as are cooking liquids, herbs and spices, and salt seasonings.

Nuts and seeds provide oil in their whole form. These become nut milk and paste or nut butter. Sesame seed paste (tahini) and almond, peanut, and cashew butters are most common. Pecan and hazelnut butter are more exotic. (Walnuts do not make a good nut butter; they are too bitter.) Nut butter is used most frequently in bean pâtés, spreads, and dips. Liquid oil from sesame seeds, olives, peanuts, corn, and safflowers is used in all the other second-stage methods that require oil.

Clarified butter, or *ghee,* is an exceptional fat to use for making croquettes and patties, unless you choose a totally dairy-free diet. It cooks well over high heat, does not soak into the beans, and makes a delicious buttery-tasting crust. To make your own, melt unsalted butter in a heavy-bottomed saucepan. When cooking more than 1 pound, allow 45 minutes of cooking at a simmer. When the milk solids have separated from the fat and they touch the bottom of the pan, yielding a golden brown color, and your kitchen is filled with the aroma of butterscotch, the ghee is ready. Remove it from the heat and strain the fat from the milk solids through a damp cotton dish towel over a strainer. Store the clarified butter in a ceramic, wood, or glass container. It will keep at room temperature for up to a month. Or refrigerate it for longer storage.

Miscellaneous Ingredients

KOMBU

ENERGETICS:
Thick, rich
COLOR:
Deep green
FAVORITE COOKING
METHODS:
All first-stage methods
NUTRITIONAL PROFILE:
Calcium, magnesium, iron, potassium, iodine, copper, zinc, vitamins

I consider this long, broad, and strong vegetable from the sea essential in bean cookery. Kombu is a natural source of glutamic acid, which in its processed form (monosodium glutamate, or MSG) is the ingredient famous in Chinese cookery for drawing out flavors of vegetables. Similarly, the glutamic acid in kombu heightens the flavor of beans. And, while I don't understand exactly how or why, beans cooked with kombu seem more digestible.

Do not use monosodium glutamate in place of kombu; better to go without. Monosodium glutamate is such an extreme, chemically produced seasoning, some people have life-threatening reactions to it. At best, one is always thirsty after a meal with MSG because the salt crystal ratio is out of balance.

Kombu has many uses, but in bean cookery it becomes part of the dish in the first-stage method. Use approximately 1 inch of dry kombu for each cup of dry beans. Kombu should be brittle. Simply snap off the size you need. Frequently I break it into small pieces so that it dissolves into the beans when they are cooked. A larger piece can be removed.

ORANGE FLOWER WATER

This liquid infusion of orange flower petals has a lighter, different taste than orange zest (the outer skin of an orange peel). Use this ingredient carefully. It clearly changes the direction of a weighty dish very easily. A little goes a long way. It is particularly useful when you want to lighten a bean dish without using too much accent liquid.

ENERGETICS:
Heavenly, arousing the senses
COLOR:
Clear
FLAVOR:
Like the scent of orange flowers in full bloom
FAVORITE COOKING METHODS:
Black Bean and Rice Croquettes, page 84
NUTRITIONAL PROFILE:
About the same as perfume (and used in about the same quantity)

HICKORY SMOKE FLAVORING

Lots of fire in this burnt wood extract makes this an intense ingredient. Anytime you want a smoky flavor, a few drops of this liquid will perform. Use it to create split pea soup without smoked ham shank or the taste of a wood fire in any bean dish.

ENERGETICS:
The intensity of war
COLOR:
Golden
FLAVOR:
Smoky, burning wood
FAVORITE COOKING METHODS:
Tempeh bacon, barbecue sauce, baked beans
NUTRITIONAL PROFILE:
Unknown

AGAR AGAR

Agar agar, a processed sea vegetable, is a gelatinlike binder that holds its shape at room temperature. It can be used to bind beans into any shape, using a form such as a bowl or gelatin mold. I use it with beans in the refry method, cooking it along with the beans and other ingredients. One bar of agar agar is enough to bind 3 cups of beans. Soak agar agar in water to cover until it is soft, press out the excess liquid, and tear it into pieces. See the recipe for Lima Bean and Kumquat Aspic on page 86.

ENERGETICS:
Magical nothingness with flexible bonding
COLOR:
Clear
FLAVOR:
None
FAVORITE COOKING METHODS:
Aspic from the refry method
NUTRITIONAL PROFILE:
None

Part II
Bean Cookery

Beans are the most important source of protein in the vegetarian diet. So, to me, the most important effort we can make in vegetarian cooking is to strive for integrity in bean cookery; then all options are open. The finesse in bean cookery lies in an awareness of when beans are properly cooked. Determining "properly cooked" is influenced somewhat by the digestive systems of people who eat them—whether beans are foreign to their bodies or attuned. To be safe, a responsible cook will take beans through all the steps of pretreatment, first-stage, and second-stage methods.

Pretreatments respond to the variables—long-, medium-, or short-cooking category, age of the bean, altitude, and cooking method. First-stage methods help the bean reach integrity; beans can then be taken into a second-stage method for final seasoning or frozen for future use. Second-stage methods bring all ingredients together to make a final dish. You cannot overcook beans. The only danger is too much or too little cooking liquid in the first stage.

PRETREATMENTS:
Soak, parboil
FIRST STAGE:
Steep, electric crock, pressure-cook, sprout, deep-fry
SECOND STAGE:
Boil, bake, marinate, refry, slow cook, blend

VARIABLES

Altitude has a major influence on how quickly and thoroughly a bean is cooked. At sea level, all cooking methods work equally well. At 5,000 feet, soaking is a requirement for all medium- and long-cooking beans unless you pressure-cook in the first stage; then soaking is only required for long-cooking beans.

Age is also a factor. An old bean (6 months to a year) could require ¼ cup more water per cup in first-stage methods. Beans more than a year old would also require a good long soak, regardless of whether it is a short- or medium-cooking bean. When beans are sold in bulk bins through an active market place, such as farmers' markets or natural food markets, it's a good bet they are not too old. There are no dates on the commercial beans sold in plastic bags in supermarkets so it is difficult to tell how long that package has been sitting on the shelf. Also, it is my experience that organically grown varieties are less resistant to yielding a good texture, where chemically grown beans are difficult to soften from time to time.

MEASURING

Measure beans before any pretreatment or first-stage cooking method when you want to control the texture. Any container will work for a measuring tool—a coffee mug, a small soup bowl, or a real measuring cup—as long as you use the same container to measure the water ratio.

In general, the ratio of liquid to beans is always to the amount of dry, unsoaked beans. Pressure-cooking unsoaked beans requires a ratio of 2½ parts water to 1 part dry beans; if soaked, pressure cooked beans require 1:1. Steeping soaked beans requires 2:1 (at sea level), electric crock cooking requires 3:1 (see the Bean Chart on page 45).

SORTING AND WASHING

Pick over the dry beans to remove stones, dirt balls, beans with worm holes, and other foreign matter. When cooking fewer than five pounds of beans, it is simplest to drop them through your hand as your eye finds the misfits and the other hand picks them out. I do this from the measuring cup into the cook pot. Larger amounts may be sorted by laying them on a table and sorting through one big batch at a time in some methodical way. Don't overlook this step. Beans are economical, but dentists are not. 'Tis the cook's duty!

Washing beans removes dust. Dead beans, ones that may be too dry, sticks, and loose dirt float to the surface during this procedure. Pour off the first batch of water without losing a bean. Wash a second and third time if necessary. There's no need to dirty a bowl; I do this right in the pot I'll be cooking in, unless they seem outrageously dirty. They should shine after their bath.

Pretreatments

Pretreatments are essential in bean cookery. They are not options. In order to benefit from what dry beans have to offer, one or more of these pretreatments must be applied to awaken the food from its sleeping state and to help the digestibility of this somewhat volatile protein. When cooking for a sensitive stomach, with the exception of sprouting, you will want to use *both* soaking and parboiling before you go into a first-stage cooking method.

Soaking

I use a simple rule: soak all medium- and long-cooking beans if you do not have a pressure cooker. (If you pressure-cook in the first stage, you only have to soak long-cooking beans.) Soaking gives the dry bean a chance to absorb water, rehydrating it. Generally, any bean will be fully soaked in 4 hours. When soaking beans longer than 4 hours or overnight, refrigerate them, especially in warm weather. After soaking, beans swell to their finished size.

Remembering to soak is the most difficult part of this pretreatment. Often we don't know until midday what dinner will be that night. Forgetting to put beans up at night shouldn't stop you from cooking them (especially if you have a pressure cooker). There are two procedures for soaking dry beans, a fast and a slow method.

Long, slow soaking is the preferred method when cooking large quantities of beans. Be sure to allow for a bowl or pot big enough to contain the rehydrated beans.

LONG SOAKING PROCEDURE
- Measure, sort, and wash the beans.
- Cover the beans with cool water at least 2 inches above the top of the beans.
- Soaking is finished when the beans are plump, somewhere between 2 and 12 hours, depending on whether they are long-, medium-, or short-cooking beans and how warm the weather conditions are. Drain (feed the soaking liquid to your plants).

SHORT SOAKING PROCEDURE
- Measure, sort, and wash the beans.
- In the first-stage cooking pot, cover the beans with cold water and bring to a rapid boil.
- Cook for 5 minutes and let rest about 1 hour. Drain.

Notice that when pressure-cooking soaked beans the cooking liquid ratio changes to 1:1.

When cooking for people with extra sensitivity to bean digestion, repeat the short soaking method two times.

SOAKING SOYBEANS

It is essential to remove the thin fibrous hulls of the soybean when pressure-cooking so that the skins do not plug the valve. After measuring and washing, cover beans with water and bring to a boil. Soak for 8–16 hours. Drain the soaking water and fill the pot again. Rub the beans through the palms of your hands to loosen the skins. They should float in the extra water. Drain and separate the hulls from the beans.

Parboiling

Parboiling is a good habit to acquire when cooking all dry beans. When soaked beans are first brought to a boil, they may give off some foam. This is good. Fast boiling for 3 to 5 minutes can help the white foamy substance rise to the top, making it easy to skim off. Without soaking, less foam rises. Unscientifically, I believe this foam contributes to the gas everyone worries so much about in bean cookery. If it can be released to the surface of the pot, we can eliminate it. So soaking and parboiling are a good combination, especially when digestive systems are sensitive.

Some beans release more foam than others, and I haven't determined what exactly causes the variables. White beans, lima beans, and split peas release more foam than black, red, and pink beans.

PARBOILING PROCEDURE
- Measure, sort, and wash the beans. Soak if desired.
- Bring the beans and kombu (1 inch per cup of dry beans) to a boil in measured liquid.
- Boil over high heat for 15 minutes.
- Skim off the thick foam that rises to the surface.
- Replace any evaporated water or liquid volume removed with foam. The beans are now ready to cook by your choice of first-stage method.

BEAN CHART FOR FIRST-STAGE COOKING METHODS

	SOAK	ALTITUDE	CROCKPOT	PRESSURE-COOK	STEEP
SHORT-TERM	Optional	<3,000 ft	3:1 – 4 hrs.	2¼:1 – 15 min.	3:1 – 30-40 min.
COOKING BEANS	1 hr.	>3,000 ft	3:1 – 5 hrs.	2½:1 – 25 min.	3:1 – 60 min.
MEDIUM-TERM	Optional	<3,000 ft	3:1 – 4½ hrs.	2½:1 – 50 min.	3-5:1 – 1½-2 hrs.
COOKING BEANS	4 hrs.	>3,000 ft	3:1 – 6 hrs.	2½:1 – 50 min.	X
LONG-TERM	6-12 hrs.	<3,000 ft	X	2½:1 – 60	X
COOKING BEANS	12 hrs.	>3,000 ft	12 hrs.	2½:1 – 60	X

SHORT-TERM BEANS	MEDIUM-TERM BEANS	LONG-TERM BEANS
Azuki	Anasazi	Chick-peas (garbanzo)
Lentils	Black-eyed peas	Black soy
Lima	Black turtle	Yellow soy
Mung	Great northern	Fava
	Kidney	
	Navy	
	Pinto	
	Red beans	

**Never use salt or salted ingredients in the first stage.

**General yield 1 cup dry = 2½ cups cooked.

**Store cooked beans in refrigerator or freezer.

First-Stage
Cooking Methods

After pretreatments, beans still are not soft enough to eat. Think of first-stage methods as the opportunity to get beans soft, preparing them for delightful dishes. The primary purpose of first-stage methods is to create the integrity of the bean—a smooth, soft, interior meat surrounded by unbroken skin. It is extremely important to have the bean achieve a state of integrity at this stage before going on to a special form or second-stage method.

Salt, salt seasonings, salt in herb and spice mixes, salt in canned tomatoes, and any hidden salts will stop the transformation of the secondary compounds. In other words, beans just don't get soft enough to be digestible with any trace of salt. Their integrity is lost. So insist that the first-stage method prepare the texture of the bean.

Kombu sea vegetable is an essential component of all first-stage cooking methods with the exception of deep-frying. I suspect that kombu, a natural form of MSG, assists in breaking down the secondary compounds and enhancing the true flavor of beans. Use it religiously in the portion of about 1 inch per cup of dry beans. It can be broken into small pieces or left whole. Small pieces will dissolve into the beans, giving you the benefits of this highly nutritional product. You may want to remove the whole piece of kombu after the beans are cooked.

Once beans are soft, they are ready to receive flavors of other ingredients. Forms, fancy flavors, shaping, and specialty dishes are all handled in the second-stage methods. The texture created in the first stage is paramount to the success of all second-stage dishes.

RULE:
No salt in first-stage methods (except deep-frying).
RULE:
Use kombu sea vegetable in all first-stage methods (except deep-frying).

COOKING LIQUID FOR THE FIRST STAGE

It is possible to use a combination of other cooking liquids with water during the first stage. Beer, wine, and sake all make interesting contributions. As long as you don't use salt, seasonings such as garlic, cumin, onion, and bay leaf enhance the taste of a first-stage bean. It may be especially good to season beans in this manner if you are planning a slow-cook dish in the second stage.

PRESSURE-COOKING:
To cook in a measured
amount of cooking liquid in a
sealed pot that holds between
15 and 17 pounds of pressure
ENERGETICS:
Strong with a steady intensity
that gently transforms the bean
FORM:
Any second-stage method

Pressure-Cooking

I live at 5,000 feet. Without a pressure cooker or Eden Foods canned beans (see page xiii), I would rarely eat beans. At this altitude, pressure-cooking is not only a great time saver, but a necessity for long-cooking beans, which have difficulty reaching integrity without pressure. Some varieties of beans, split peas for example, are not suitable for pressure-cooking. Be sure you know your ingredients before you try this method. The Bean Chart (page 45) will guide you.

Don't think of pressure-cooking beans as a blasting job. Instead, know that when properly used, a pressure cooker holds beans in a gentle constant pressure. Some pressure cookers do a little dance on top when the pressure is up. With too much fire, this could feel violent. But when the pressure is held under optimum fire, it is silent and energetically held. As long as you have enough liquid and not too much liquid, beans can stay in the pressure cooker for hours. Vicki proved this theory by accident. One day, she set the beans to pressure-cook, brought the pressure up, turned down the flame, set the flame tamer in place, and after some time left the house to go to town. For Vicki, town is forty miles away. Six hours later, she returned to find the beans still held carefully under pressure and cooked to perfection. The water to bean ratio must have been right. Too much water and the beans would have been split open.

PROCEDURE

- Place pretreated beans in the pressure cooker.
- Add a measured amount of cooking liquid with no salt (see the Bean Chart for ratios). Add kombu (about 1 inch per cup of beans).
- Bring to a boil for 3 minutes. Skim off any foam that rises and can be caught. Replace any cooking liquid removed with the foam (this can be as much as a ½ cup).
- Seal the pot and bring to pressure. Take care that the seal is in place and the top does not leak any steam or water out the side of the cover.
- Set a flame tamer under the cooker (even on an electric stove). Time the cooking from when the pressure has come to full intensity. Turn the heat down to maintain a constant pressure, around medium to medium-low. There should be little or no sound nor obvious activity from the pressure cooker.

- After the allotted cooking time, bring the pressure down by running cold water over the top of the pot until the safety release valve has gone down and there no longer is pressure in the pot. Most modern pressure cookers will not open until the pressure inside the pot has been reduced to a safe opening point.

Steeping

I like to distinguish between "boiling" and "steeping" because to me boiling is a method that requires much more liquid than is required to actually cook the bean. I think of boiling as a method for making soup. Steeping suggests that we use just enough liquid to cook the beans so that should we want to make something other than soup, the character of the beans is not lost into the broth.

Some people think it is easier to control the texture of the bean while steeping. This may be true, especially at sea level. At sea level, steeping is a reasonable first-stage cooking method for beans. It is possible to steep at higher altitudes when the beans are fresh, soaked, and of the short-cooking variety.

Use a pot large enough for expansion and one that has a good seal to avoid losing too much steam or liquid while cooking. A heavy bottom will keep the beans from scorching. On occasion, more cooking liquid will need to be added during cooking. This should be hot.

PROCEDURE
- Measure, sort, and wash the beans.
- Place in a heavy pot with a measured amount of cold cooking liquid (see Bean Chart for ratios). Add kombu (1 inch per cup of dry beans).
- Bring to a boil for 3 minutes. Skim if necessary and replace any lost liquid.
- Cover; reduce the heat to medium-low with flame tamer.
- Cook until soft. Make sure there is enough water to cover the beans at all times; add hot water as necessary.

STEEPING:
To cook on the stove top in a pot with a cover so that all the cooking liquid is used up in creating a bean with integrity
ENERGETICS:
Slow, attentive, balanced
FORM:
Any second-stage method

ELECTRIC CROCK
COOKING:
To cook in an electric crock
made for off-the-stove cooking
ENERGETICS:
Long, slow, gentle
FORM:
Any second-stage method

Electric Crock Cooking

Even though Harriet told me it was possible, for ten years I couldn't believe that an electric slow cooker would actually be able to create a soft enough bean at the altitude I live. Then one day I walked into Ester's house and smelled beans, and my nose led me right to her Crockpot. This pot had created beans with a fabulous integrity without concern. The ease of this method is very attractive. The only drawback is the length of time it takes beans to actually cook. But they will cook, except long-cooking beans, such as garbanzos and soybeans.

PROCEDURE

- Place the pretreated beans in the slow cooker.
- Cover with a measured amount of cold cooking liquid and kombu.
- Place on the high temperature setting for at least 3 hours.

Reduce to low if leaving the house or cooking overnight. Make sure beans are very soft before adding salt (see Bean Chart on page 45 for timing).

Sprouting

SPROUTING:
To transform the internal
structure of a bean without
fire, through air and moisture
ENERGETICS:
Graceful, demanding
FORM:
Marinating, refrying

Sprouting is not really a cooking method, since no fire is involved. But it functions as a first-stage method, breaking down the secondary compounds of dry beans. Instead of heat, sprouting uses water and air to tease the bean's own reproductive system to engage in growth.

As a bean sprouts, it grows a tail. Each kind of bean grows a different length of sprout. In mung beans it is as if the sprout is eating the bean and the seed itself disappears into a long tail. This is an example of a fully transformed bean sprout, one where it is obvious that those secondary compounds aren't in a position to attack your digestive system because they have already spent their energy doing something else. Other beans you may have seen or heard of as sprouts, including garbanzos, lentils, soybeans, and sometimes whole dry peas, are less likely to spend enough energy to distract the secondary compounds. So in my mind they need to be cooked in a second-stage method.

Usually when preparing your own sprouts it is important to purchase special sprouting seeds. This is not essential; it simply guarantees more yield per spoonful of sprouts and fewer misfits. But the seeds do have to be whole and young.

PROCEDURE

- Wash beans with lukewarm water.
- Place the beans in a bowl or large jar and cover them with warm water measuring about 3 times their depth. Secure a top with cheesecloth, a fine mesh screen, or a sprouting top (found in health-food stores). Place the jar in a warm, dark place and let the beans soak for 8 to 12 hours for short-cooking beans and 12 to 24 hours for medium- and long-cooking beans.
- Drain the beans and spread them evenly against the edges of the jar or bowl. Replace the cover. Keep warm, moist, and dark.
- Rinse the beans 3 to 4 times a day. Drain thoroughly each time.
- After 4 days, uncover the sprouts, allowing them indirect light. Continue to rinse and drain as the tail grows. The sprout should be between 2 and 3 inches in length.
- Eat quickly.

Deep-Frying

Deep-frying is probably the most unusual first-stage method for beans. Where other first-stage methods are only a means to a second-stage dish, deep-frying beans is an end in itself, best known in the delicious, crunchy bean balls called falafel. Using the creative process allows many variations on this traditional dish.

Deep-frying is not as unhealthy as some would think, conjuring up a vision of gobs of fat dripping off the food. It is oil-intensive, but most of the oil is left behind in the pan. The quality and temperature of oil regulate how good this dish will be. Refined, saturated oils have created a problem for people when used in this cooking method. Deep-frying in oil that is too cold saturates the food even if you use unrefined oil. Only use safflower or canola oil. These oils, even if they are unrefined, can attain a high enough heat without bubbling over the pot. Maintain a temperature of 375°F when deep-frying. Add more food to cool the oil rather than adjusting the flame. Keep an even flow of items going in and out of the oil to maintain the temperature. Use a pot that will allow at least 2 inches above the oil because as beans enter the oil rises. In the beginning there are many fast moving bubbles. Watch out; they also raise the oil level.

Usually more oil is attracted to the deep fried food when salt or sweeteners are added to the dish before frying. But in the case of deep-fried beans, it is better to add the salt to the bean dish before cooking.

DEEP-FRYING:
To cook soaked, ground, and shaped beans quickly with seasonings in a large amount of oil (more than will be absorbed by the dish)
ENERGETICS:
Hot, fast, intense
FORM:
Croquette, side and main dish, appetizer

This cooking method feels best on cold windy days or when your body seems dry and stoic. It's a good technique to know about for those passionate moments in crisp fall or winter.

RULE: When the oil is too cool, it saturates the food. When it's too hot, it burns the food. When it's just right, a light crust surrounds your dish with no excess oil offering even a drip.

Deep-frying as a first-stage cooking method requires that beans are pretreated by soaking. It is difficult to deep-fry beans when they have been cooked first without a massive amount of grain to bind them. Cooked rice, soaked bulgur or couscous, cornbread crumbs, and cooked millet all become options for a twosome croquette. But a true bean dish of the deep-fry method requires simply soaking and grinding.

PROCEDURE

- Soak the beans and drain them of all liquid. Let them rest.
- Blend or mash the beans to an even consistency. Thirty to 60 seconds in a food processor should do it.
- If using cooked beans, add a small amount of binder, such as bread stuffing, pretzels, or cracker made into a medium-fine powder. Don't use flour; it makes the croquette pasty.
- Add baking powder and any spices, herbs, or decorative vegetables.
- Form the beans into an appropriate shape. My most recent favorite design for cooked beans is first shaped into a log about 1″ by 1″ or 1″ by 2″ and then is pressed flat.
- Heat the oil until it begins to move, shimmering across the surface.
- Carefully place the shaped beans into the oil and cook on both sides until golden brown and cooked through. Remove with a wire skimmer or slotted spoon, let drain for a few seconds over the oil, and place on something to drain. Don't remove extra oil from the bean as it leaves the pot.

Falafel

1 cup dry garbanzo beans
3 cups water
2 teaspoons garlic granules
3 teaspoons ground cumin
1 teaspoon red pepper flakes
¾ teaspoon aluminum-free baking powder
1½ teaspoons vegetable salt
¼ to ½ cup fresh cilantro, minced

Traditionally falafel are served with a tangy sesame tahini and lemon sauce. In theory I would consider this a redundant use of oil, but because it is absolutely delicious and it is fixed in history as a companion sauce with fresh lettuce and vegetables, I highly recommend serving these bean balls with tahini sauce.

Serves 4-6

1. Soak the beans in water for at least 8 hours. Drain thoroughly.

2. Chop the beans in a food processor for 30 seconds. Add the garlic, cumin, red pepper, baking powder, vegetable salt, and cilantro and blend for another 30 seconds or until evenly blended.

3. Shape the bean mixture into little balls, pressing firmly toward the center and smoothing them out at the edges by rolling them around in your hands.

4. Heat oil to 375°F. Deep-fry the balls a few at a time until they are crisp on the outside and even color on the inside, about 5 minutes.

SERVING SUGGESTIONS: Pita bread, lettuce, tomatoes, cucumber, and tahini dressing flavored with lemon or mint makes this a traditional dish. Or consider placing the balls in a hot sauce and serving over freshly cooked grain.

The Process

BEANS: Other beans and tofu and tempeh work in this style of dish. The ratios are the same for the other ingredients. I liked this with white beans.

OIL: Safflower can be replaced with canola oil. Don't try any other unrefined oil. It won't work.

SALT SEASONING: Vegetable salt makes a multidimensional contribution. Plain sea salt is a good alternative. Other salt seasonings would change the texture, adding too much moisture. Normally salt is left out of the deep-fry method because it attracts too much oil. But in this case, without salt, the beans are not fully cooked and taste flat. The extra oil is modest in relation to the delicious potential of this dish.

HERBS AND SPICES: There are many options in this category from spicy to aromatic. For palates that like a fiery experience, red pepper flakes turn up the heat. More exotic tastes may use cumin or cardamom. Cinnamon may suggest a donut-eating experience, and culinary herbs, such as dill, tarragon, or basil, make a light but full-bodied taste. Fresh herbs, such as cilantro or parsley, help to color the dish as well.

VEGETABLES: These little balls need to be tight to survive the hot oil treatment. If you do use some decorative vegetable such as green onion or red pepper, mince it very fine so that the edges won't keep the bean from holding on to itself.

PRETREATMENT:
Soak
FIRST STAGE:
Deep-fry
BEANS:
Garbanzo
OIL:
Safflower
SALT SEASONING:
Vegetable salt
HERBS/SPICES:
Garlic, cumin, cilantro, red pepper
VEGETABLES:
None

French Lentil Balls

1 cup French green lentils
3 cups water
4 teaspoons dry tarragon
4 teaspoons dry basil
¾ teaspoon aluminum-free
  baking powder
1 teaspoon sea salt
Safflower oil for deep-
  frying

Make sure you use French green lentils. They are smaller and darker green than the regular green lentil. Together with basil and tarragon, they give this dish a distinctly different ambiance than traditional falafel. This dish makes a good appetizer or company for a sauce.

Serves 4–6

1. Soak the lentils in water for at least 4 hours. Drain thoroughly.

2. Blend the lentils in a food processor for 30 seconds. Add the tarragon, basil, baking powder, and sea salt and blend another 30 seconds or so.

3. Shape the mixture into little balls about ½ inch in diameter or larger balls about 1 inch in diameter.

4. Heat the oil to 375°F and add the balls. Cook until crispy on the outside and even colored on the inside, about 5 minutes. Remove and drain on paper towels.

SERVING SUGGESTIONS: Dip into tahini sauce or serve as "meatballs" with pasta in tomato sauce.

The Process

PRETREATMENT:
Soak
FIRST-STAGE:
Deep-fry
BEANS:
French green lentils
OIL:
Safflower
SALT SEASONING:
Sea salt
HERBS/SPICES:
Basil, tarragon
VEGETABLES:
None

BEANS: Yes, other beans also work in this method.

OIL: Safflower and canola work well together or interchangeably.

SALT SEASONING: Sea salt can be replaced or enhanced with vegetable salt. Other salt seasonings will change the texture of the mixture and, with the exception of miso or umeboshi paste, could make it too wet.

HERBS AND SPICES: The herbs in this particular version of deep-fried beans keep the character aromatic. Other suggestions are fresh parsley, rosemary, dill, oregano, and thyme.

VEGETABLES: These little balls need to be tight to survive the hot oil treatment. If you do use some decorative vegetable, such as green onion or red pepper, mince it very fine so that the edges won't break up the bean's continuity.

Tahini Dipping Sauce

My version of this sauce is somewhat tangier than the restaurant versions I have sampled. Thanks to umeboshi vinegar, this dish has a kick and is a digestive aid to the tender bean croquettes. This sauce is still worth making even if you don't have umeboshi vinegar; just increase the amount of lemon and salt.

Yield: ½ cup (2–3 servings)

Mix all ingredients together in a blender or food processor. Store in the refrigerator.

2 or 3 large cloves garlic, minced
3 tablespoons raw tahini (ground sesame paste)
3 tablespoons umeboshi vinegar
4 tablespoons lemon juice
¼ cup water

Salsa Dipping Sauce

Based on the Mexican salsa used to spice up bean and corn dishes, this is only one version. So when your bean balls aren't hot enough, use this spicy sauce to raise the temperature. In some cases it is served along with the tahini sauce. This is a large batch. Store it in the refrigerator.

Yield: 6 cups (24 servings)

Mix all ingredients well; chill. Let rest for several hours to set flavors.

4 cups (28 ounces) canned crushed tomatoes
1 tablespoon olive oil
1 tablespoon garlic granules
1 tablespoon cumin
1 tablespoon oregano
1 tablespoon red pepper flakes
1 cup V-8 juice
1½ cups fresh ripe tomatoes (optional, use only if very ripe)
½ cup fresh cilantro, minced
1 cup water
1 to 2 teaspoons sea salt

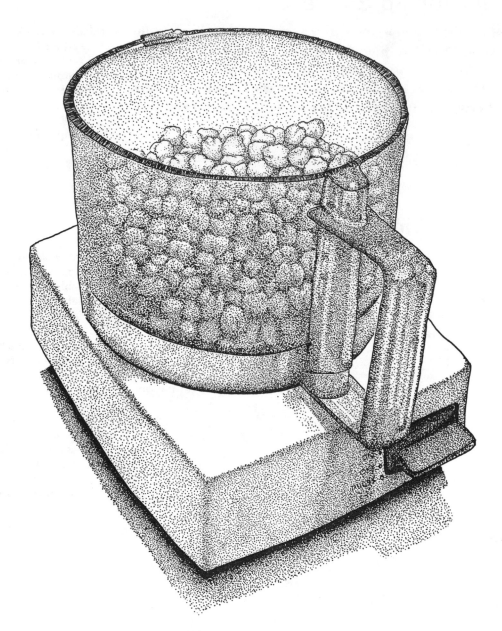

Second-Stage
Cooking Methods

Baking

Baking beans that are already soft is a wonderful way to enhance them. Whether in a casserole or a pâté, beans can bake for many hours, allowing you freedom to do other things. A dish that will bake in an hour at 350°F can take 6 to 8 hours to bake at 200 or 250 degrees. Choose a combination of temperature and timing that suits your needs.

BEAN PÂTÉS

Bean pâtés are simple, yet they allow a myriad of taste experiences. They age beautifully in the refrigerator, peaking in about three days to a week. This form gives you great opportunity to arrange flavors that become one outstanding taste. Serve them on vegetables or crackers, as a sandwich filling, or as company for salads.

First, and most important, the first-stage beans must have integrity. If they are too wet, the pâté will run. If the beans are too firm, they won't blend or digest properly. Ideally you want the pâté to hold its shape after baking, and this depends solely on the integrity of the bean in the beginning. Sometimes you will need to strain beans from their bean juice, whether you prepare them in the first stage or purchase beans in a can. If the pâté is too runny you can add bread, cracker, or pretzel crumbs (but then I call it a loaf).

Pâtés are flavored by vegetables, herbs and spices, a choice of nuts or nut butter, and salt seasonings. In my style of cooking, these ingredients cannot simply be blended and served as pâté; they must also be baked to integrate the flavors and then pressed to expel extra moisture and shaped into the pâté form. The technique of pressing condenses a somewhat puffy and expanded dish. Special pâté baking pans include an insert for this purpose, the diameter being slightly smaller than the baking dish. But you can easily improvise a baking and pressing assembly (see Procedure).

A pâté will bake from 1 to 3 hours at 350°F, depending on how many vegetables are blended into the beans. In winter, I bake the pâté overnight at 250°F. During classes, I hurry it through at 400°F for 1 hour, but this is definitely not the preferred method. Bean pâtés like to be baked slowly.

BAKING:
To prepare beans in combination with salt seasoning, oil, herbs and spices, and vegetables and cook with heat surrounding the pot, usually in the oven
ENERGETICS:
Held in the arms of even, steady heat
FORMS:
Casserole, pâté/loaf

PROCEDURE

- Determine if the beans have enough integrity to make a good pâté. You might need some bean juice to adjust the texture, especially if the beans have been drained, refrigerated, or frozen.
- Either by hand or in a food processor, chop the onions and other vegetables and herbs to a fine texture.
- In either a blender or food processor, blend the beans with the chopped vegetables until they are quite smooth. Look for a texture like that of wet clay.
- Blend in the salt and oil. The taste should be less salty than you desire at the finish, because baking reduces the liquid and intensifies the salt taste.
- Adjust the taste as needed with additional herbs and spices. The flavors should be somewhat strong and distinct; you will notice different tastes bouncing all over the place. That is expected until flavors have been integrated by cooking.
- Correct the texture if needed. Too dry? Add more oil or accent liquid. Too wet? Add bread crumbs. The texture should be a cross between heavy, wet sand and thick pudding.
- Select a deep baking dish with a pressing object, such as a plate, board, or brick, that will fit easily in the opening of the baking dish. A glass or ceramic soufflé dish works well with a small salad plate; a loaf bread pan works with a brick wrapped in food quality paper or foil, but something like a fish poacher is ideal.
- Oil or butter the inside of the baking dish and pour the bean mixture into it. Butter some foil on the shiny side. Place that buttered side facing the beans and seal loosely, allowing some head space. You may prefer oven-proof plastic between the foil and the beans. The beans expand and may raise as much as 2 inches above the edge of the pot, depending on how much is in the dish; they will sink again as they cool.
- Bake until there is a slightly crisp edge on top and at the sides of the dish. In a moderate oven (350°F), allow 1½ to 2 hours; in a hot oven (400°F), 1 hour; and in a slow oven (225-250°F), 6 hours.
- Remove the pâté from the oven. Place the pressing object on top of the foil. Find a steady weight (about 5 pounds) to put on top, such as a gallon of water or beans, a flour bin, or a rock. Let cool at room temperature for 1 to 3 hours.

- Insert a knife around the edges of the baking dish. Invert a serving plate over the top of the pâté. Lift the pâté pan and plate simultaneously and flip together as the pâté leaves the pan.
- Wrap the pâté tightly and store in the refrigerator up to two weeks, or freeze.

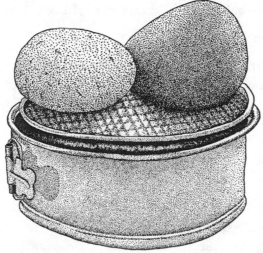

CASSEROLES

Think of this style of baking beans as a bunch of beans bound by a sauce, possibly with accompanying vegetables in either a decorative or major capacity. Famous dishes in this style of bean cookery are Boston baked beans, lasagna, and the French *cassoulet* (the last, traditionally made with pork, lamb, and Italian sausage, is a good example of how beans were considered vegetables instead of protein). Most casseroles are composed of beans, vegetables, and a sauce, and are baked uncovered to achieve a lovely crust.

Another favorite form of casserole uses a pastry crust to surround a savory mixture as it bakes. Look for several examples of this style of dish in the Tofu and Tempeh Cookery chapter beginning on page 127; some of them are suitable for bean fillings as well.

PROCEDURE
- Preheat the oven; oil or butter a baking dish (optional).
- Assemble first-stage cooked beans, raw or sauteed vegetables, sauce, and any other ingredients.
- Determine whether you will cover the baking dish or not.
- Bake until the surface has a light brown crust. Serve hot or warm.

1 tablespoon ghee
   (optional)
1½ cups cooked navy
   beans, with juice
½ cup onion, diced
¾ cup barbecue sauce
   (see page 147)
1 cup Ivy chicken-style
   seitan (optional)
¼ teaspoon sea salt

Boston Baked Beans

This is probably the easiest recipe in the book: little navy beans cooked in your favorite barbecue sauce. Seitan adds texture and bulk to an easy-to-overeat bean dish. Make sure you use a non-porous baking dish; you want all the juices to stay together.

Serves 3–4

Preheat the oven to 350°F. Mix the ingredients in a baking pot. Cover and bake for 1 hour. Uncover for the last 15 minutes to achieve a crust.

SERVING SUGGESTIONS: This is a side dish to go with polenta, pasta salad, rice, millet, or quinoa as well as a cooked vegetable dish.

The Process

FIRST STAGE:
Electric crock
SECOND STAGE:
Bake (casserole)
BEANS:
Navy
COOKING LIQUID:
Bean juice, barbecue sauce
OIL:
Ghee (optional)
SALT SEASONING:
Sea salt
HERBS/SPICES:
Barbecue sauce
VEGETABLES:
Onions

BEANS: Any white bean will work in this dish.
COOKING LIQUID: Barbecue sauce makes the cooking liquid. Change the sauce for variations. Watch how the dish changes all together. Compare this process with the Garbanzo Beans With Root Vegetables (page 66). Notice the similarities.
SALT SEASONING: Just a pinch of salt helps integrate all the flavors and completes cooking the beans. Other salt seasonings are not appropriate.
OIL: Oil isn't necessary, but it gives the dish a golden crusty tan at the edges. If you use anything, use ghee or safflower oil.
HERBS AND SPICES: The barbecue sauce has plenty of spice and flavor, so nothing extra is needed. If you change the sauce, consider orange zest and cinnamon in addition to barley malt, ginger, and horseradish.
VEGETABLES: Just onion, the essential bean companion.

Red Beans in Chili Sauce

Southwestern flavors meet to make this an exquisite side dish.

Serves 4-6

1. Preheat the oven to 350°F. Combine the beans, onions, tomatillos, tomatoes, and sweet corn in a baking dish with a cover.

2. Heat a skillet or sauce pan over medium-low heat. Add the oil, garlic, chili powder, garam masala, and corn meal. Cook and stir for 3 minutes.

3. Add the water and bean juice slowly, stirring with a whisk to avoid lumping. Add the salt and cook just until the sauce is established in substance.

4. Stir the sauce into the beans. Cover and bake until all the flavors are fully integrated, 30 to 45 minutes.

SERVING SUGGESTIONS: This is a great side dish for any grain and good company for corn or wheat tortillas and a fresh salad.

1½ cups cooked kidney beans, drained (reserve juice)
1 cup onion, diced
1½ cups fresh tomatillos (green tomatoes), husked and quartered
4 tablespoons canned tomatoes, crushed
1 cup fresh sweet corn (optional)
2 tablespoons corn oil
1 tablespoon chopped garlic
2 tablespoons chili powder
¼ teaspoon garam masala
2 tablespoons cornmeal
1½ cups bean juice (add water if needed to make 1½ cups in all)
1 teaspoon sea salt

The Process

BEANS: Red kidney beans are plump and colorful in this dish. Pinto, Anasazi, small red, and black turtle are all good choices to substitute for kidneys and still keep a similar taste and character with the chosen flavors.

COOKING LIQUID: Bean juice is the cooking liquid. If your beans don't have any extra juice with them, consider using wine or beer with water to create the sauce that the beans bake in. Or soak dried sweet corn and use its liquid.

SALT SEASONING: Plain sea salt keeps the color and flavors clear and light. If you use a lighter bean, such as pinto, consider what tamari or dark miso would do to the color and weight of the dish. Umeboshi would only be appropriate in small, accent-liquid quantities. Sea salt is the best choice to integrate flavors. When you have a combination of vegetables and spices, as in this dish, you want the flavors of those ingredients to come together without the distraction of a flavored salt seasoning.

OIL: Corn oil was chosen to host the fresh corn and cornmeal. But olive or safflower oils would be acceptable alternatives.

FIRST STAGE:
Electric crock
SECOND STAGE:
Bake (casserole, flour sauce)
BEANS:
Red kidney
COOKING LIQUID:
Bean juice, water
SALT SEASONING:
Sea salt
OIL:
Corn oil
HERBS/SPICES:
Garlic, chili powder, garam masala
VEGETABLES:
Onions, tomatillos, tomatoes, sweet corn

HERBS AND SPICES: Garlic, chili powder, and garam masala make a direct taste without being excessive. Cumin, coriander, and cilantro could also be added, but, again, I like compositions to be fairly uncomplicated where each ingredient weighs significantly, like the lines of a Zen painting.

VEGETABLES: Onions, a given in bean dishes, should only be replaced by a member of the onion family, such as leeks, shallots, or green onions. Fresh corn and tomatillos make this bean dish light and seasonal. Frozen corn might be a substitute choice, but get the best tasting corn you can find. Good dry sweet corn tastes like candy.

Black Bean Pâté

Deep and delicious, the flavors in this dish are strong. You could easily shift the theme of this dish to Southwestern flavors by replacing peppercorns with mild roasted green chili peppers.

Serves 15

2 shallots
2 cups green onions, coarsely cut
¾ cup cilantro
1 cup white onion, diced
2 teaspoons green peppercorns
3 cups cooked black beans, drained
6 tablespoons tahini
4 tablespoons red miso
¾ cup dry-roasted pumpkin seeds

1. Preheat the oven to 350°F.

2. In a food processor, blend the shallots, green onions, cilantro, and onions into the finest pieces possible. Add the peppercorns and blend them to a coarse cut. Add the beans, tahini, miso, and blend until smooth. Add the pumpkin seeds and blend to a coarse cut.

3. Butter a pâté baking dish (see page 58) and fill it with the bean mixture. Spread it evenly. Cover with buttered foil or ovenproof plastic wrap. Bake until a light golden crust surrounds the edges, 1½ to 2 hours.

4. Remove the pâté from the oven when the crust has formed. Place the inside plate over the pâté and add a weight (about 5 pounds). Let cool at room temperature, then refrigerate. Will keep for two weeks or longer in the freezer.

SERVING SUGGESTIONS: Spread very thinly on a tortilla, water cracker, or fresh vegetable and serve as an appetizer; or use as sandwich filling.

The Process

BEANS: Any bean is a good choice in this basic pâté.

COOKING LIQUID: None; you don't want to dilute the substance. If the beans are too dry, moisten lightly, using bean juice whenever possible.

SALT SEASONING: Red miso was chosen both to match the color of the bean puree and for its delicious fermented flavor, which helps the bean pâté age over time into a ripe, full, delicious taste.

OIL: I first tried this dish with black olives as the oil and the salt, but they gave off a bitter taste. So I now fall back on tahini, my standard oil for pâté. Consider almond or filbert butter.

HERBS AND SPICES: Cilantro acts as an herb, while green peppercorns provide the spice. Of course these can be changed, but you will have to rely on the smell and taste test (page 15).

VEGETABLES: Combining three members of the onion family— shallots, green onions, and white onions—allows their flavors to work together offering a variety of tastes without changing the overall direction of flavors.

FIRST STAGE:
Pressure-cook
SECOND STAGE:
Bake (pâté)
BEANS:
Black turtle
COOKING LIQUID:
None
SALT SEASONING:
Red miso
OIL:
Sesame tahini, pumpkin seeds
HERBS/SPICES:
Shallots, cilantro, green peppercorns
VEGETABLES:
Green onions, white onions,

Black-Eyed Pea, Apricot, and Pecan Pâté

2 shallots
8 whole dried (moist) Turkish apricots, diced
2 cups cooked black-eyed peas
2 tablespoons raw sesame tahini
2 tablespoons white miso or chickpeaso
½ cup pecans
1 tablespoon amaretto

This is probably the most exciting of all the dishes that were created for this book. It is so very delicious it is dangerous. Unlike other pâtés, this one must be served warm. And take time to chew it. I can't emphasize enough how much better it will taste if you let it linger in your mouth, letting the taste buds have full reign of pleasure.

Serves 6–8

1. Preheat the oven to 350°F.

2. In a food processor, mince the shallots. Add in the apricots, black-eyed peas, tahini, and miso and blend until smooth. Add the pecans and amaretto and chop them coarsely.

3. Oil or butter a pâté baking dish (see page 58). Pour the bean mixture into the baking dish. Cover it with buttered foil or oven-proof plastic wrap. Bake until the beans expand and brown slightly, about 2 hours. Weigh, cool, and store as directed on page 59.

SERVING SUGGESTIONS: Serve a dollop in a triangular wedge of cool red pepper, either as an appetizer or with a salad.

The Process

FIRST STAGE:
Electric crock
SECOND STAGE:
Bake, pâté
BEANS:
Black-eyed pea
COOKING LIQUID:
Amaretto
SALT SEASONING:
White miso
OIL:
Pecans, tahini
HERBS/SPICES:
Shallots
VEGETABLES:
Apricots

It is rare that I find a dish so perfect that I can't see options clearly. This is one of those dishes.

BEANS: Black-eyed peas have a gorgeous off-peachy-tan color. They were the inspiration for reaching for the apricots.
COOKING LIQUID: The beans were a little dry, so I was perusing my miniature liquor collection and landed on amaretto. Its sweet nutty-fruity flavor was a perfect match.
SALT SEASONING: Not wanting to destroy the soft color of the already chosen ingredients, I chose sweet white miso to enhance the direction of this dish.
OIL: With such elegant Southern flavors, pecans seemed to be the most suitable oil.
VEGETABLES: Apricots replace vegetables in this variation of pâté. Choose plump, moist apricots rather than leathery, dry ones.

Lentil, Tarragon, and Caper Pâté

You will probably need to be fond of capers to truly love this tangy and smooth pâté. If you don't care for them, refer to the vegetable section of the process to change this ingredient.

Serves 10-20

1. Preheat the oven to 350°F.

2. Heat a large skillet and add the oil and sliced mushrooms. Cook over high heat until mushrooms are fully cooked, brown, golden, and fairly dry.

3. Peel the onion and shallots and mince in a food processor. Add the nuts and blend until smooth. Add the lentils, umeboshi paste, and tarragon and blend until evenly mixed. Add the capers and mushrooms and chop coarsely.

4. Place the mixture in an oiled pâté pan (see page 58). Cover with buttered foil, and bake for 1½ hours.

5. Remove the pâté from the oven, place the pressing plate on top of the pâté, add a weight, and cool at room temperature.

SERVING SUGGESTIONS: This pâté would do well as a thin spread on a thin cracker for an hors d'oeuvre or as company for a salad. Or try it as a sandwich filling or stuffing material for leafy greens, pasta, or peppers. Or simply prepare a grain dish and serve with the warm pâté.

1 tablespoon canola oil
1 pound fresh mushrooms, sliced
1 medium onion
3 shallots
1 cup cashews (raw or roasted)
3 cups cooked lentils, drained
4 tablespoons umeboshi paste
1½ tablespoons dry tarragon
3 tablespoons capers

The Process

BEANS: Any bean will do. But lentils are light in color. So pay attention to color, and taste with the other ingredients if you are changing the bean.

COOKING LIQUID: If the pâté mixture seems dry before you bake it, use a little of the caper juice as an accent liquid (it is sour and salty), or liquid umeboshi vinegar in place of paste. At least use a little bean juice, but avoid water—you don't want to dilute the flavors.

SALT SEASONING: Umeboshi paste is the primary salt seasoning in this dish, but capers are also salty. They add an extra bit of salt as well as the accent. Definitely try this dish with miso.

OIL: I used roasted cashews for this pâté, but I trust that raw cashews would also be good. Tahini and pecan butter are alternate choices.

FIRST STAGE:
Pressure-cook
SECOND STAGE:
Bake (pâté)
BEANS:
Lentils
COOKING LIQUID:
None
SALT SEASONING:
Umeboshi, capers
OIL:
Cashews, canola

HERBS/SPICES:
Tarragon, shallots
VEGETABLES:
Capers, onions, mushrooms

HERBS AND SPICES: Tarragon and shallots represent the herb and spice category. Garlic and basil would be good alternates.

VEGETABLES: Capers, delicate pickled flower buds, are tangy, salty bursts of flavor. Neither fruit nor vegetable, this ingredient fills the categories requirement. Mushrooms and onions deepen the flavor but also create more moisture for this otherwise dry assembly of ingredients. Roasted red pepper or reconstituted dried tomatoes make an outstanding substitute for the mushrooms.

Garbanzo Beans With Root Vegetables

2 tablespoons peanut oil
1 cup leek (one medium), cut into 1½-inch chunks or owl cut (see illustration)
1 cup carrot (one medium), cut into 1½-inch chunks or owl cut
1 cup turnip (one medium), cut into 1½-inch chunks
1 cup rutabaga (one medium), cut into 1½-inch chunks
1½ cups cooked garbanzo beans, drained (reserve juice)
2 cups garbanzo bean juice and/or water (room temperature or cold)
4 tablespoons rice flour
1½ teaspoons sea salt
2 cloves garlic, chopped (optional)
1 bay leaf

An all-time favorite, there are many variations on this dish. It seems to work with multiple vegetables and singular vegetables. This recipe is very simple and easy to make. The key to the success of this dish is the cut of the root vegetables and taking time to seal their edges. Notice that this recipe and Red Beans in Chili Sauce (p. 61) use flour-thickened sauces. Stay away from pure wheat flour sauces; they become gluey in texture and dull the flavors. If you have to use wheat flour, you also need to increase the salt seasoning, herbs, and spices.

Serves 4-6

1. Preheat the oven to 350°F.

2. Heat a skillet over medium-high heat. Add the oil and leek. Toss the leek to lightly coat the edges with oil and then don't move it for a few minutes; the idea is to sear the walls gently, browning them. Add the carrot, toss, and let the edges brown, turning occasionally. Repeat with the turnip and rutabaga, taking time for each one to seal. Don't add more oil. This will take about 15 or 20 minutes.

3. Remove the vegetables from the skillet and place them in a baking pot with a good lid. Add the drained garbanzo beans.

4. Beat the rice flour and bean juice in a bowl or cup until evenly moistened. Pour it into the skillet and stir quickly over medium heat until the sauce thickens. While stirring, add salt, garlic, and bay leaf.

5. When the sauce has come into balance, mix it with the beans and vegetables. Cover and bake for 45 to 50 minutes. Adjust the seasoning with tamari if needed.

SERVING SUGGESTIONS: Any grain dish and salad make good company for this sumptuous dish. It is best served hot.

The Process

BEANS: I suspect any bean would love baking in this sauce.

COOKING LIQUID: Use whatever juice you have from cooking the garbanzo beans. Sometimes there just isn't enough bean juice to make up the quantity of cooking liquid required for the sauce. Water is the best choice to keep this dish focused. The root vegetables offer so much flavor by themselves, sometimes it is best to let that through. Water will do that. A touch of white wine could work on this meaty style bean, but it could also throw it off into a bitter fashion. Use a good quality wine or mirin.

SALT SEASONING: Plain sea salt brings the flavors together in a most direct way so use it to transform the dish. Other salt seasonings, such as umeboshi, shoyu, or miso, would be lovely to add at the end if the dish isn't sweet enough or feels incomplete.

OIL: Ghee is magnificent in this dish. Dark sesame oil also gives good quality and flavor. If you have to use a less flavorful oil, like canola, consider an interesting salt seasoning or garlic to make up for its lack of character.

VEGETABLES: This is always the hardest selection for me to make in this dish. Often, I simply choose only one from what is at hand. When perusing a healthy produce market I enjoy composing from a group of interesting relationships around bitter, salty, and sweet natures. For example, try sweet roots like carrots and parsnips, with earthy burdock and celeriac; or with sweet squash, use bitter brussels sprouts, rutabaga or turnip, or perhaps a spot of hot daikon radish. Select only three. Well, *maybe* five. And always something from the onion family.

FIRST STAGE:
Pressure-cook
SECOND STAGE:
Bake (casserole, flour sauce)
BEANS:
Garbanzo
COOKING LIQUID:
Bean juice, sauce
SALT SEASONING:
Sea salt
OIL:
Peanut oil
HERBS/SPICES:
Bay leaf
VEGETABLES:
Leek, carrots, turnips, rutabagas

Owl cut (left); diagonal half-moon cut (right)

SLOW COOKING:
To simmer first-stage cooked beans gently in an open or covered pot with a selection of cooking liquid, vegetables, herbs, spices, a salt seasoning, and sometimes an oil or a sauce
ENERGETICS:
Steady, slow, and sweet integration of flavors
FORM:
Side dish

Slow Cooking

Slow cooking, a very simple method, relies on low fire, for a long time. Its purpose is to create truly sweet flavors that rise out of beans when salt has been cooked into the dish. Most frequently this style of dish is used as a side to grain dishes, where ¼ to ½ cup is enough for a serving. Both major and decorative vegetables work in chorus with slow-cooked beans. If you are not measuring, just add enough liquid to cover the beans. They don't need extra because they are already cooked. Too much liquid will dilute their taste. Notice that if you add more cooking liquid, you would have soup.

PROCEDURE

- Heat a heavy-bottomed pot. Add oil, herbs or spices, and vegetables and cook until the edges of the vegetables are sealed and they no longer feel raw.
- Add the cooked beans, salt seasoning, and enough cooking liquid to almost cover.
- Cover and cook over low heat with a flame tamer for 15 minutes to 1 hour. The beans will be done in 10 minutes, but if you are using root vegetables the dish may need more time. Sometimes the longer they cook, the better they are.
- Adjust the taste with salt seasoning.

Curry Lentil Lush

1 tablespoon olive oil
2 cups chopped leeks
6 cloves garlic, chopped
1 cup carrot, ¼ moon cut
1 tablespoon dry basil
1 tablespoon crushed
   fennel seed
6 clove stems, crushed

One day when I was feeling particularly odd, I stumbled upon this combination of flavors. I even used curry, which I normally dislike. But the color drew me in and the taste brought me to appreciate the Old World rye bread that accompanied this dish. Even though Lentil Lush was designed as a side dish, you could add more cooking liquid and make it a soup.

Serves 6-8

1. Heat a heavy-bottomed pot and add the oil. Add the leeks and garlic and cook slowly, sealing the leeks until they are clear and somewhat brown. Add the carrots, basil, and spices and continue cooking

until sealed. Allow 10 to 15 minutes to slowly seal these vegetables and herbs.

2. Add the lentils, vegetable juice, water, bouillon cube, curry powder, lemon zest, bay leaf, and vegetable salt.

3. Bring to a slow boil and simmer for 30 minutes. Remove the lemon peel before serving.

SERVING SUGGESTIONS: Serve with toasted caraway pita bread for lunch or with a rice and vegetable dish for dinner.

The Process

BEANS: These ingredients and technique work well with any medium cooking bean. White beans tend to prefer sweet flavors, so try this with lima, great northern, or cannellini beans.

COOKING LIQUID: A combination of vegetable juice, vegetable stock (bouillon), and bean juice contributes to the complete flavor of this dish. If you don't have vegetable juice at hand, water will do, but then you will want to increase the amount of herbs and spices and probably salt.

SALT SEASONING: Vegetable salt offers another chance to bring dimension to the cooking liquid. Especially when cooking with only one vegetable, I like to use Spike, which has about forty ingredients in it. Plain salt with tamari would be good alternatives.

OIL: Olive oil keeps this a fruity taste as well as offering a thorough browning of the vegetables, creating a stronger flavor in the vegetable stock base.

HERBS AND SPICES: Variations on the sweet spice theme are cinnamon, cardamom, and nutmeg. The color of this dish could be shifted a bit by adding turmeric or curry powder if you like those flavors.

VEGETABLES: Carrot is the only vegetable in this dish other than the leeks. There is almost always a member of the onion family in a bean dish. So they almost don't count as a vegetable. Use a regular onion if you don't have leeks. More vegetables are possible, but with the complex flavors from the herbs and spice category it is probably best to keep this one simple.

---

2 cups cooked lentils, drained
2 cups vegetable juice (combination of tomato, carrot, celery, parsley; or use V-8)
2 cups water
1 cube vegetable bouillon (salted Morga)
2 teaspoons curry powder, or to taste
5 or 6 strips lemon zest (large enough to remove)
1 bay leaf
1 teaspoon vegetable salt (Spike)

FIRST STAGE:
Steep
SECOND STAGE:
Slow cook
BEANS:
Lentils
COOKING LIQUID:
Water (bouillon), vegetable juice
SALT SEASONING:
Spike, bouillon
OIL:
Olive oil
HERBS/SPICES:
Garlic, basil, fennel, clove, curry
VEGETABLES:
Leeks, carrots

Simple Azuki With Leeks

2 teaspoons dark sesame
  oil
1 cup leeks, slivered,
  green and white
  together
½ cup carrot, diced
2 cups cooked azuki
  beans, drained
¼ teaspoon sea salt
1 cup sake
1 tablespoon tamari

This dish is a good example of how a simple cooking method honors the bean. No additional herbs or spices detract from the flavor of azuki beans, but vegetables arouse the taste buds for the whole dish. Treat the ingredients kindly. Each one counts.

Serves 4–6

1. Heat a heavy-bottomed pot over medium-high heat. Add the oil and leeks and cook until leeks are wilted and bright, about 2 minutes. Add the carrots. Cook for 10 minutes until they are sealed and deeper in color.

2. Add the beans, salt, and sake. Cook for 10 minutes or longer. Add tamari to taste and serve warm.

SERVING SUGGESTION: Delicious with a dish of millet pressure-cooked with diced cauliflower (see Millet Mash in *Amazing Grains*) or a simple rice dish. A leafy green salad would complete the meal.

The Process

FIRST STAGE:
Pressure-cook
SECOND STAGE:
Slow cook
BEANS:
Azuki
COOKING LIQUID:
Sake
SALT SEASONING:
Tamari, sea salt
OIL:
Dark sesame
HERBS/SPICES:
None
VEGETABLES:
Leeks and carrots

BEANS: Any bean will do. But pick ones of distinct taste because they are really the featured ingredient in this style of dish.

COOKING LIQUID: Sake (Japanese rice wine) lifts the weight of azuki beans to a place of pleasure. This liquid reduces slowly, keeping the beans from drying out and making a saucy gravy out of all the ingredients. Wine, mirin, or beer could also make this a worthy dish.

SALT: Notice I have used two salt seasonings: plain sea salt to enhance the flavor of beans as they cook and integrate with the vegetables, and tamari to finish the taste. Umeboshi or miso may also work, but if you use miso, dilute it with the cooking liquid. Use your taste and smell sensors when combining salt seasonings.

OIL: Dark sesame oil adds more to the simplicity of this dish than would an oil with less character. Using a plain oil would demand more ingredients, such as ginger or bay leaf. But any will do, because the main function of oil here is to enhance the vegetables so that they make good companions with the beans.

VEGETABLES: Leeks are the major vegetable, while carrots are decorative. Other root vegetables, such as turnip, burdock, beets, and especially rutabagas, are possibilities as major or decorative vegetables. But use only one.

Black-Eyed Peas in Rosemary and Lemon

Mary Bowman brought this simple but full-flavored combination of ingredients to my attention. It is best served warm or hot soon after cooking, while the extra liquid still surrounds the beans.

Serves 4

Combine the black-eyed peas, lemon zest, rosemary, wine, water, and salt in a sauce pan. Heat thoroughly and cook for 10 minutes. Add tamari to taste. Serve hot.

SERVING SUGGESTIONS: This is a side dish. Rice, couscous, millet, quinoa, or buckwheat would love to share the plate with this bean dish. Include a major vegetable dish.

2 cups cooked black-eyed
   peas, drained
1 tablespoon lemon zest
1 teaspoon fresh rosemary,
   minced
⅛ cup white wine
   (optional)
½ cup water
Salt to taste
Tamari to taste

The Process

BEANS: Other beans, such as navy or garbanzo, are acceptable with the ingredients of this recipe.

COOKING LIQUID: Mirin can replace wine or both can be replaced by water.

SALT SEASONING: Sea salt helps integrate the flavors and sweeten the beans, and tamari shifts the taste dimension slightly, rounding off the flavors. You could use umeboshi or miso in place of tamari. Make sure to use the taste and smell test to determine which style of miso works best.

OIL: Because there are no vegetables to seal, no oil is required in this dish.

HERBS AND SPICES: Rosemary is a dominant herb; everything it touches holds its flavor. Lemon zest, just the oil-bearing outer layer of the lemon peel, accents and lightens the heaviness of the beans and the natural intensity of rosemary. (Don't include the white part of the peel; it will make your dish bitter.) Use alternate combinations, such as cilantro and lime, or sage and apple cider vinegar.

VEGETABLES: There are no vegetables in this particular dish, not even onions. The beans stand out more.

FIRST STAGE:
Pressure-cook
SECOND STAGE:
Slow cook
BEAN:
Black-eyed pea
COOKING LIQUID:
White wine, water
SALT SEASONING:
Sea salt, tamari
OIL:
None
HERBS/SPICES:
Rosemary, lemon zest
VEGETABLES:
None

Black Beans With Garlic and Cilantro

1½ cups cooked black
   beans (1 can Eden)
¼ cup red wine (preferably
   Merlot)
1 tablespoon garlic,
   chopped
¾ teaspoon sea salt
Tamari to taste
¼ cup minced cilantro

Deep, dark, and inviting, this dish draws you in to the mystique of beans. It is extremely easy and can easily be a bean lover's staple.

Serves 3

1. Combine the beans, wine, garlic, and salt in a heavy-bottomed saucepan. Cover and cook for at least 20 minutes on medium-low heat. Use a flame tamer on gas stoves or if you have a thin-bottomed saucepan.

2. Add cilantro and tamari before serving.

SERVING SUGGESTIONS: Serve hot next to rice, millet, or cornbread, and as company to a wildly colorful vegetable dish.

The Process

FIRST STAGE:
Pressure-cook
SECOND STAGE:
Slow cook
BEANS:
Black turtle
COOKING LIQUID:
Red wine
SALT SEASONING:
Sea salt, tamari
OIL:
None
HERBS/SPICES:
Garlic, cilantro
VEGETABLES:
None

BEANS: Any bean will work for this cooking method but you will have to judge the taste and color of other ingredients as you shift the bean.

COOKING LIQUID: A white bean may do better with mirin or a white wine as the cooking liquid, and a tan bean with beer. Water may be substituted as well.

SALT SEASONING: Depending on the final color of your dish, you may want to include tamari. This is especially true if you are using water as the cooking liquid, because tamari gives that fermented wine-like flavor. Should you use tamari, you could reduce the amount of sea salt.

OIL: No oil is needed.

HERBS AND SPICES: Garlic could be eliminated or replaced with onion and hot chilies. Cilantro could be eliminated or replaced with basil, fennel, or cumin.

VEGETABLES: The dish was designed without vegetables to accompany a major grain and major vegetable as a side dish. Should you wish to add vegetables, slow cook them first, add the beans and other ingredients, and slow cook them together.

Lima Beans With Tomato and Corn

Lima beans command simplicity. In this very straightforward dish, they share the stage with fresh corn as a decorative vegetable and tomatoes for a great saucy base.

Serves 4

Combine all ingredients in a heavy-bottomed saucepan and cook for 20 minutes.

SERVING SUGGESTION: Serve with toasted herbed bread and creamy squash or carrot soup.

1 teaspoon olive oil
½ tablespoon garlic
½ cup crushed tomatoes (canned or fresh)
2 cups cooked lima beans, drained
¾ teaspoon sea salt
½ cup (1 ear) fresh sweet corn kernels

The Process

BEANS: Garbanzo and kidney beans would be a good alternative for this very simple recipe.

COOKING LIQUID: No extra liquid is required beyond what comes from the tomato juice.

OIL: Sesame oil would make a good alternative to olive oil. Ghee is always an option.

SALT SEASONING: Plain salt is best. Light miso is a possibility, but use a touch of sea salt anyway, because light miso is not very salty.

HERBS AND SPICES: Garlic is the only influence in this category. Other herbs could be included or substituted: dill, oregano, basil, fennel, cilantro, or garam masala.

VEGETABLES: Potatoes, rutabaga, and turnips can be added to the corn and tomatoes, but they need to slow cook on their own for 15 to 25 minutes before they are ready to receive the beans.

FIRST STAGE:
Electric crock
SECOND STAGE:
Slow cook
BEANS:
Lima
COOKING LIQUID:
Tomato juice, bean juice
SALT SEASONING:
Sea salt
OIL:
Olive oil
HERBS/SPICES:
None
VEGETABLES:
Tomatoes, sweet corn

Curried Garbanzo Beans With Spinach

⅔ cup coconut milk
1⅓ cups garbanzo bean juice or water
3 tablespoons unbleached white flour
½ cup (2 large) shallots, diced small
2 teaspoons curry powder
1 teaspoon sea salt
1½ cups cooked garbanzo beans, drained (reserve juice)
½ tablespoon lemon juice
4 cups (½ pound) spinach washed, dried, cut small

This dish, a great example of how one can reproduce a dish from another place without having seen or tasted it, came to me through Nerina from Nyoden, the *tenzo* (kitchen person) at the Dai Bosatsu Zendo in upper New York State. Nerina explained a dish that she had liked from her stay at the Zendo. Like a detective, I asked her questions so that I could formulate the cooking method, cooking liquid, herbs and spices, and combination of main ingredients. After visualizing all these elements, I chose to use the following ingredients, composing the dish to respond to Nerina's dietary guidelines. Later I received the original cook's ingredient list and matched the similarities and differences, which are revealed in the Process section of this recipe.

Serves 4–6

1. Combine the coconut milk, bean juice or water, and flour in a saucepan or skillet. Stirring, heat until the flour binds without lumps and makes a sauce consistency.

2. Add the shallots, curry powder, and sea salt. Mix thoroughly and add the beans. Cook over a medium heat for 10 minutes.

3. Five minutes before serving, add the lemon juice and the spinach. Serve when the spinach is bright green.

SERVING SUGGESTIONS: Serve warm over a hot bed of grain or pasta. I suspect that a kasha dish would be good in the winter and quinoa or rice would be great any time.

The Process

PRETREATMENT:
Soak
FIRST STAGE:
Pressure-cook
SECOND STAGE:
Slow cook
BEANS:
Garbanzo

BEANS: The beauty of using garbanzo beans in this dish is how they stand out individually. I can't think of another bean that offers such a creamy, individual character while not interfering in the color scheme. Black beans would be gorgeous against a white sauce, perhaps with red swiss chard as the leafy green. Make sure the beans are cooked yet whole to make the best of the color contrast. It still could bleed some. Nyoden suggests tofu.

COOKING LIQUID: Nyoden used bean juice. In the case of the garbanzo bean and curry combination, the colors work well using garbanzo bean juice and, believe me, there is nothing like the flavor that it creates in a dish. Bean juice from black beans or red beans would dominate the color. But using coconut milk in addition to the major cooking liquid adds oil and a soft flavor. If I hadn't used a nut milk, I would have sealed the shallots and curry in some olive or sesame oil, because a flour sauce such as this requires oil. Other nut milks are also a possibility. Almond and filbert milks have a clean feel and would be good alternatives in this dish.

SALT SEASONING: Tamari and shoyu make great alternative or additional salt seasonings for this dish. In fact, tamari was the salt seasoning used in the Zendo, but Nerina asked to have the dish without soy, so salt alone did the job. In combination with sea salt, miso or umeboshi could be included in this dish.

OIL: Coconut milk provides oil for the dish. See Cooking Liquid for how to alter the oil. Nyoden used olive oil, I suspect to bind the powdered herbs and spices in preparing the flour sauce.

HERBS AND SPICES: Nerina also requested low-potency spice in her food. She had the most divine curry powder in her cupboard, so a little served the dish well. This recipe is mild compared to the excitement Nyoden presented. She used garlic, yellow mustard, cumin, coriander, garam masala, curry, and a pinch of chili pepper. That should give you some great ideas on where to go with the flavor.

VEGETABLES: If spinach is not your choice, Swiss chard hosts a similar character. Although it is herbal in nature, I think fresh cilantro would make a lovely decorative vegetable, against carrots as a major vegetable. Nyoden recommended onions, cauliflower, and even potatoes.

COOKING LIQUID:
Bean juice, coconut milk
SALT SEASONING:
Sea salt
OIL:
Coconut milk
HERBS/SPICES:
Shallots, curry
VEGETABLES:
Spinach

Frijoles Borrachos (Drunken Beans)

4 cups cooked pinto beans
1 bottle (12 ounces) beer
2½ cups bean juice
2 teaspoons sea salt
1 teaspoon crushed cumin
 seed
4 cloves garlic, minced
2 cups diced onion
1 tablespoon oil (optional)
¼ teaspoon hickory
 smoke flavoring
 (optional)

Ester Rebman shared her family's secrets for preparing this traditional American Indian dish, where beans float comfortably in a bath of tasty liquid. "The crock pot, water, beans, just a few cumin seeds, an onion, and garlic, that's all. Salt goes in the final stage of cooking and sometimes some *piloncillo* (Mexican-style raw sugar) to sweeten the dish. Oh yes! Don't forget a piece from a ham hock." Well, I will forget the ham hock and match it with hickory flavoring and good oil. Instead of feeling a need to replace the flavors meat offers, you can increase the amount of vegetables, herbs, and spices, although beans usually speak for themselves when properly cooked.

This is one dish where the first and second stage seem to flow together. You cook the beans until done, then add the other ingredients and cook some more to integrate the flavors.

Serves 8

Combine all ingredients in a heavy-bottomed pot or Crockpot. Cook for several hours, until all flavors are one.

SERVING SUGGESTIONS: Serve with fresh, refried rice or wheat tortillas.

The Process

FIRST STAGE:
Electric crock
SECOND STAGE:
Slow cook
BEANS:
Pinto
COOKING LIQUID:
Bean juice, beer
SALT SEASONING:
Sea salt
OIL:
None
HERBS/SPICES:
Garlic, cumin
VEGETABLES:
Onions

BEANS: Pinto beans could be replaced with similar styles such as anasazi, bolita or tepary.

COOKING LIQUID: Bean juice and beer make up the volume for bathing these drunken beans. If you rely mostly on water, increase the herbs/spices, salt seasoning, and vegetable contributions.

SALT SEASONING: Sea salt is the most efficient ingredient of this category when it comes to large quantities of very simple ingredients. Some tamari would be acceptable as a finishing taste.

OIL: Oil is not necessary, but usually a little makes a dish more romantic. Choose canola to avoid interfering with the established taste.

HERBS AND SPICES: Cumin and garlic can be embellished with oregano, chili powder, or bay leaf. Or, add a whole jalapeño chili, and remove it before serving.

VEGETABLES: Onion can be joined by other members of its family, such as leek or shallot. Other vegetables don't really fit.

Refrying

This second-stage method is so famous, it's available in a can. When you buy refried beans in a can, they have been blended and heated with salt and oil. You can reheat them without oil and season them with herbs and spices, a sweetener, and a salt seasoning or serve them plain. But plain is not what *Romancing the Bean* is about, so I want to give you some ideas on what to do with this second-stage bean dish, whether canned or homemade.

In addition to the spreadable refried bean form, variations on this cooking method include patties and aspics. Patties are bound by either cooked grain or cracker, bread, or pretzel crumbs. Aspics are held in a vegetable gelatin called agar which, unlike animal gelatin, will gel and hold its shape at room temperature (see Lima Bean and Kumquat Aspic, page 86).

REFRYING:
To reheat cooked beans (whole, shaped, blended, or mashed) in a skillet with oil, herbs, spices, and decorative vegetables
ENERGETICS:
Quick, thorough
FORM:
Patties, aspics, and side dishes

REFRIED BEANS PROCEDURE

- Heat the skillet over medium-high temperature. (Preheating the skillet allows the oil to cover the surface quickly, requiring less oil than if it were put into a cold pan.)
- Add a small amount of oil, enough to lightly seal the vegetables.
- Add herbs and spices to the oil. (Oil will carry the flavor of the spices to other ingredients.)
- Add the decorative vegetables, sealing them with the oil.
- Mash or blend first-stage cooked beans before adding them to the skillet; or if you prefer, you can mash them in the skillet with a large spoon or potato masher. Add salt seasonings and other miscellaneous ingredients.
- Mix the ingredients and cook slowly over medium-low heat until the flavors blend, approximately 15 minutes. Cover the skillet when beans appear dry.

REFRIED BEAN PATTIES PROCEDURE

- Combine whole cooked beans, cooked grain, decorative vegetables, and herbs and spices in a large bowl. Taste for balance of seasonings.
- By hand, press the mixture into a shape for refrying. Adjust the texture so that it will hold its shape while cooking: if too dry, add a little liquid; too soft, add more binder.
- Heat a skillet and add oil. Add the patties and cook slowly and thoroughly to a crisp edge on all sides.

Azuki Beans With Sweet Rice and Plantain in Grape Leaves

2 teaspoons safflower oil
1 medium plantain, cut on diagonal ⅛ inch thick
⅛ cup sweet red pepper, diced small
1 tablespoon fresh lemon balm, minced
1 cup cooked sweet rice
½ cup cooked azuki beans
1 tablespoon tamari
6 to 8 brined grape leaves, soaked or rinsed

This unusual appetizer style dish was inspired from many directions: a gift of fresh lemon balm from Kathy; memories of a dish of sweet rice, banana, and black beans rolled in banana leaf from the oriental market; remembrance of my Puerto Rican college roommate who introduced me to plantain; a current experience from an appetizer party I catered with a tropical theme; and a dish from an improvisation class, which left me with first-stage sweet rice decorated with red pepper. Unlike most refried bean dishes, the beans in this dish are not mashed, but refried whole with the grain. This dish uses beans as a decorative concept.

Yield: 6–8 rolls

1. Heat a skillet over medium-high heat. Add the oil and sliced plantain. Cook on both sides until crisp.

2. Remove the plantain slices from the skillet and add the red pepper, lemon balm, rice, and beans, taking time to heat each thoroughly before adding the next. Take care not to mash the beans.

3. Add tamari and cook for 2 minutes.

4. Open a grape leaf. Dip it in cold water. Place it vein side up. Lay a crisp plantain or two as a strip vertically down the middle on top of the grape leaf.

5. Place a tablespoon of rice and beans on top, log-shaped, and wrap the leaf around the grain as illustrated.

SERVING SUGGESTIONS: Serve warm or at room temperature. You may reheat them by steaming them briefly. Try them as a snack or party appetizer.

The Process

BEANS: Black beans, French green lentils, and tepary beans are also the right size for this presentation, and they all offer a distinct color difference from the rice.

COOKING LIQUID: Not required. However, you could replace the tamari with a small amount of an accent liquid made from salty and sour ingredients, such as vinegar with diluted miso or vinegar with plain salt. See the Braising chapter of *Amazing Grains* for more ideas.

SALT SEASONING: Umeboshi vinegar or diluted miso would both work in place of tamari. Straight salt would not work in this second-stage method because there isn't any cooking liquid to dilute it. Salt needs to be either diluted and transformed over heat or beaten into oil or liquid vigorously by hand.

OIL: Hazelnut or light sesame oil would be good alternates.

HERBS AND SPICES: Fresh lemon balm could be replaced with another herb or left out altogether. Ginger, cardamom, or hot pepper are some ideas. Again, just use one if possible.

VEGETABLES: Plantain is critical to the uniqueness of this dish. I haven't found any acceptable substitute because it becomes very crisp and sweet, yet is compatible with the other ingredients. Red peppers, the decorative vegetable in this dish, are here mostly for their color contrast to the grain. Other decorative vegetables (parsley, red radish, green onions, etc.) could be included, but don't add too many.

FIRST STAGE:
Pressure-cook
SECOND STAGE:
Refry (with grain)
GRAIN:
Sweet rice
BEANS:
Azuki
COOKING LIQUID:
None
OIL:
Safflower
SALT SEASONING:
Tamari
HERBS/SPICES:
Lemon balm
VEGETABLES:
Grape leaves, plantain, sweet red peppers

Black Bean Burritos
in Green Chili Sauce

SEITAN FILLING
    (optional)
1 pound Ivy Foods Hearty
    Wheat Original Seitan
1 tablespoon olive oil
2 tablespoons sherry wine
    vinegar
½ teaspoon black pepper
¼ teaspoon sea salt

BEANS
3 tablespoons corn oil
2 cloves garlic, minced
1 cup onion, diced
4 cups cooked black
    beans
2 teaspoons sea salt, or
    to taste

SAUCE
7 to 10 canned roasted
    and peeled green chilies
3 cups water
1½ teaspoons vegetable
    salt, or to taste
1 teaspoon rice vinegar
3 tablespoons arrowroot
    flour
½ cup fresh cilantro, cut
    small (optional)

6 large wheat flour
    tortillas

In this dish, Mexican-style refried beans are rolled in tortillas and baked in a flavorful sauce. An optional ingredient in the filling is seitan, a wheat-based protein that resembles meat in texture, but surpasses it in taste.

Serves 6

1. Slice the seitan into ¼-inch strips 2½ inches long. Combine with the oil, vinegar, pepper, and salt in a 3-quart bowl and mix very well. Add the seitan strips and let sit 1 hour, tossing occasionally.

2. For a crisper texture, heat a little more oil in a skillet and brown the seitan slightly. Chop medium-fine in a food processor.

3. Preheat the oven to 350°F. For the bean filling, heat a skillet over medium-high heat. Add the corn oil, garlic, and onion and cook until the onion is somewhat golden on the edges. Puree half the beans and add to the skillet with the whole beans. Add salt to taste and refry until the flavors integrate.

4. For the sauce, blend the chilies in a blender or food processor to a texture somewhere between chunky and smooth. Combine in a saucepan with the water, salt, vinegar, and arrowroot. Heat and stir until the cloudiness disappears. Stir in the cilantro.

5. Spread ⅓ to ½ cup refried beans over each tortilla. Lay ground seitan on top and roll into an open-ended cylinder. Place seam side down in a 9 × 13-inch baking dish. Repeat with the remaining tortillas. Pour the sauce over the burritos, cover, and bake for 30 minutes.

SERVING SUGGESTIONS: Serve with a clear soup and an avocado salad.

The Process

BEANS: Any whole bean will do.

COOKING LIQUID: Seitan is marinated with the accent liquid wine vinegar. This could also be lime juice or rice vinegar. The green chili sauce relies on water, but you could substitute a soup stock or add a vegetable buillon cube, especially if you don't use vegetable salt as the salt seasoning.

SALT SEASONING: Plain sea salt is used throughout this three-part dish, except that vegetable salt flavors the plain water of the green chili sauce. In a multidimensional way, it keeps the sauce clear where tamari or miso would shift the color and clarity.

OIL: Relatively little oil is required in this dish. Cooking the seitan before grinding and baking it is optional. If you do refry the marinated seitan, use olive or corn oil, whichever you have used in refrying the beans.

HERBS AND SPICES: Notice there are not too many extraneous herbs and spices in this dish. The full flavor comes from the beans and the chilies. Cilantro is optional, but can be used either in the beans or in the sauce.

VEGETABLES: Onions and chilies romance the bean in this main dish. Other vegetables need to accompany it through a soup, salsa, side dish or salad.

FIRST STAGE:
Pressure-cook
SECOND STAGE:
Refry
BEANS:
Black turtle
COOKING LIQUID:
None (in the beans)
SALT SEASONING:
Sea salt
OIL:
Corn oil
HERBS/SPICES:
Garlic
VEGETABLES:
Onions

Black-Eyed Pea Patties

1½ cups black-eyed peas,
   drained
½ teaspoon garlic powder
1 teaspoon sea salt
¼ cup (approximately)
   cracker or pretzel meal
¼ cup cilantro, minced
5 tablespoons ghee

This is an example of how very simple but delicious a dish can be. If you like it more elaborate, you can add decorative vegetables or your choice of spices.

Serves 2–4

1. Blend the beans, garlic, salt, and ¼ cup cracker meal into a paste. Add the cilantro and shape into small patties. Roll patties into additional crumbs for variation and more stability.

2. Heat a skillet over medium heat and melt the ghee. Lay the patties in the skillet and cook slowly until the edges brown, 3 to 5 minutes per side.

SERVING SUGGESTIONS: Serve these morsels on a plate with both a grain and a cooked vegetable dish.

The Process

FIRST STAGE:
Electric crock
SECOND STAGE:
Refry (patties)
BINDER:
Cracker crumbs
BEAN:
Black-eyed peas
COOKING LIQUID:
None
SALT SEASONING:
Sea salt
OIL:
Ghee
HERBS/SPICES:
Garlic powder, cilantro
VEGETABLES:
None

BEANS: Black, pinto, red, navy, lima, or kidney beans all make good possibilities for this dish.
COOKING LIQUID: None.
SALT SEASONING: If you think the dish needs more salt at the end of cooking, sprinkle tamari upon the patties while they are still in the skillet. Exchange sea salt for vegetable salt.
HERBS AND SPICES: Fresh cilantro is hard to pass up, unless you are one of the many people who have difficulty enjoying this unusual herb. Basil, or even a touch of rosemary or sage, would be alternate possibilities. Garlic is the only member of the onion family, so don't let it go.
VEGETABLES: Red peppers or green onions, minced ever so fine, could be added to a dish like this as decorative vegetables.

Tepary Potato Patties

I don't expect many of you to be able to find tepary beans in your local market, but the day may come. These small beans, actually a whole group of heirloom varieties which have been grown in the Southwest and northern Mexico for about 5,000 years, come in an array of colors, from white to gold to brown and black, or speckled with blue. (The name, by the way, comes from the early Spanish explorers; when they asked the Papago people what they were eating in 1699, the Indians responded, *"T'pawi,"* meaning, "It's a bean.") I would love to see them become more widely available, but in the meantime, this recipe will work fine with Anasazi or pinto beans.

Yield: about 10 cakes (serves 4)

1 cup cooked golden tepary beans, drained
½ teaspoon epazote leaves, crushed
½ cup leek, slivered
1 teaspoon sea salt
½ cup russet potatoes, grated
½ teaspoon black pepper
⅓ cup fine white cracker crumbs
2 to 4 tablespoons ghee
1 tablespoon Grand Marnier (optional)

1. Combine the beans, epazote, leek, and salt in a food processor and blend thoroughly to a smooth spread. Add the grated potatoes, pepper, and cracker crumbs and mix by hand. The mixture should be a thick, heavy batter.

2. Heat a large heavy skillet over medium heat and melt half the ghee. Add the bean mixture by large spoonfuls, making the size and shape you desire. Cook uncovered, turning once, until the patties form a crust, 5 to 10 minutes on each side. Reduce the heat to medium-low; do not cover. Turn, adding the remaining ghee as needed. Taste one to make sure the potato is cooked.

3. (Optional) Sprinkle ¼ teaspoon of Grand Marnier over the finished patties.

SERVING SUGGESTIONS: Miniatures make good finger food for parties. Larger patties could be an entree served with both a cooked and a raw vegetable dish.

The Process

BEANS: Pinto, Anasazi, and kidney beans are possible choices to substitute for tepary beans. Make sure they are not cooked in too much liquid in the first stage; it could alter the dish too much.
COOKING LIQUID: None, unless you want to use the Grand Marnier for the finishing touch.

FIRST STAGE:
Pressure-cook
SECOND STAGE:
Refry (patties)

BINDER:
Cracker crumbs
BEANS:
Golden tepary
COOKING LIQUID:
Grand Marnier
SALT SEASONING:
Sea salt
OIL:
Ghee
HERBS/SPICES:
Pepper, epazote
VEGETABLES:
Potatoes, leeks

SALT SEASONING: Plain salt is the best ingredient to integrate these simple flavors. If you find it needs a little more salt after cooking, a dash of tamari or umeboshi would improve the taste.

OIL: Ghee allows the refried patties to cook without excessive oil. You can combine some of a flavorful oil, such as sesame or olive, with the ghee to achieve a crustier surface.

HERBS AND SPICES: Epazote is a potent Mexican herb with an odd, dramatic flavor, to be used in small portions. A single other herb would also work, such as cilantro, fennel, basil, or tarragon. Pepper is important to give a kick to this group of somewhat dense textures.

VEGETABLES: Potato could be replaced with winter squash or carrots. Leeks could be replaced by any other member of the onion family.

1 cup cooked black beans
1 cup cooked brown rice,
  room temperature
¼ cup sweet red pepper,
  diced
1 glove garlic, minced
¾ teaspoon sea salt, or
  to taste
⅛ teaspoon orange flower
  water
¼ teaspoon garam masala
4 tablespoons white
  cracker crumbs
2 to 4 tablespoons ghee
1 small green onion,
  slivered
Fresh lime wedges as
  garnish

Black Bean and Rice Croquettes

Even though these savory, sturdy croquettes are great traveling food, they are best served fresh and hot. Don't ignore the lime juice garnish; this ingredient makes the senses go wild.

Serves 3–4

1. Combine the beans, rice, red pepper, garlic, salt, orange flower water, garam masala, and 2 tablespoons of the cracker crumbs together in a bowl. Mix to a coarse texture, but try not to mash the beans.

2. Shape the mixture into 6 or 8 circles or flattened logs. Combine the remaining 2 tablespoons of cracker crumbs and the green onion. Lightly toss and press the croquettes into the crumbs, making sure a few green onion pieces stick also.

3. Heat a large heavy skillet over medium-high heat. Add half of the ghee and all the croquettes. Cook on one side until a crust has formed, add the remaining ghee, and turn to cook on the second side.

4. Serve hot with lime wedges.

SERVING SUGGESTIONS: These patties go well in a meal with a multi-vegetable soup and a crisp salad.

The Process

BEANS: Any bean will do, but carefully consider how it may combine with the subtle flavors of orange and garam masala. Think of the variations on this style of bean and grain dish as a chance to use different beans with different grains: for example, red beans with wehani rice, white beans with white rice, or garbanzo beans with corn bread, which would take the place of both the cracker crumbs and the rice.

COOKING LIQUID: Orange flower water provides a scent to lighten the weight of beans and rice. It takes your taste buds on a journey. If you change the herbs and spices, you may want to alter this ingredient or eliminate it.

SALT SEASONING: Plain sea salt helps integrate the multiple flavors in this dish. I wouldn't confuse this delicate balance with a more complex salt seasoning.

OIL: Ghee, my favorite oil for cooking this form of beans, treats the croquettes gently and requires much less quantity than other oils.

HERBS AND SPICES: Garam masala and garlic work well, giving dimension to the plain rice and beans. Other herbs and spices would also work with garlic, but check them against the cooking liquid with the taste and smell test (see page 15).

VEGETABLES: Red bell pepper acts as a decorative vegetable, but it also contributes its distinctive sweet taste. Well cooked, diced carrots or green onions are also options.

FIRST STAGE:
Pressure-cook
SECOND STAGE:
Refry (patties)
BINDER:
Cooked brown rice
BEANS:
Black turtle beans
COOKING LIQUID:
Lime juice, orange flower water
SALT SEASONING:
Sea salt
OIL:
Ghee
HERBS/SPICES:
Garam masala
VEGETABLES:
Sweet red peppers

Lima Bean and Kumquat Aspic

4 inches agar bar
½ cup water
1 cup cooked lima beans
4 plump fresh kumquats
2 tablespoons mirin
¼ cup fresh-squeezed
   orange juice
1 teaspoon sea salt
¼ teaspoon white rice
   vinegar

This daring dish, one of the most unusual compositions in this book, truly romances the lima bean. The sweet and tart orange flavors give a dramatic relish to the basically bland flavor of the beans. Serve it in small quantities in a multicourse meal.

This really isn't a refried dish, since there is no oil involved, but it otherwise uses the same technique as the other refried bean recipes.

Yield: 4 2-ounce ramekins (serves 4)

1. Soak the agar bar in ½ cup water for 10 minutes. Meanwhile, blend the lima beans, kumquats, mirin, orange juice, salt, and vinegar to a smooth spread.

2. Carefully remove the agar from the water and squeeze out the extra water. Tear the agar into small pieces and add it to the beans and blend until it is part of the mixture.

3. Heat a heavy skillet over medium heat and cook the beans for 10–15 minutes, covering to avoid loss of liquid. Stir occasionally.

4. Pour the beans into four 2-ounce ramekins or one 8-ounce bowl and let it set up at room temperature or in a refrigerator. Store in refrigerator.

5. (Optional) When ready, insert a butter knife between the beans and the bowl, inverting it to slide upon a serving plate.

SERVING SUGGESTION: Serve as a spread for bread or crackers or as a component of salad on a bed of green leaves.

The Process

BEANS: Lima beans and kumquats create a strong bond. I don't think any other bean would respond to this combination of ingredients.

COOKING LIQUID: Unlike most refried bean dishes, this form requires some extra liquid for the agar to cook in. Orange juice and mirin accent the sweet fruity character of this dish, while balancing the bitter kumquat with their sweetness. The small amount of rice vinegar challenges these opposite flavors, bringing the dish to completion. If served with a ginger dressing, all five tastes will be included.

SALT SEASONING: Plain sea salt integrates the variety of flavors best without confusing the dish.

OIL: None.

HERBS AND SPICES: There is no need for anything from this category in the recipe. Ginger would be a good addition, in small quantities.

VEGETABLES: Kumquats, a bitter fruit, star in this dish. There are no supporting fruits or vegetables, no alternatives.

FIRST STAGE:
Pressure-cook
SECOND STAGE:
Refry (aspic)
BINDER:
Agar
BEANS:
Lima
COOKING LIQUID:
Mirin, orange juice, rice vinegar
SALT SEASONING:
Sea salt
HERBS/SPICES:
None
VEGETABLES:
Kumquat
OIL:
None

Mexican Refried Beans

1 tablespoon rich,
    unrefined corn oil
1 to 3 cloves garlic,
    minced
1 cup diced onion
½ cup diced green pepper
2 teaspoons mild chili
    powder
3 cups cooked pinto
    beans, with juice
1 teaspoon sea salt
2 teaspoons rice syrup
Tamari or shoyu to taste
    (optional)

This dish is traditionally very simple, but I have embellished it a bit. Don't be misled by the other ingredients; it's the taste of the beans that counts.

Serves 6-8

1. Heat a skillet over medium-high heat and add the oil, garlic, and onions. Cook until the onions are transparent. Add the green pepper and chili powder, mix well, and cook for 3 minutes.

2. Mash or blend the beans with their juice to a combined texture of smooth and whole beans. Add them to the vegetables. Add the salt and rice syrup and cook for 10 minutes, or until all the flavors have integrated. Stir regularly. If the flavor needs a little more salt, adjust with tamari or shoyu.

SERVING SUGGESTIONS: Use as filling for corn or flour tortillas, as a dip for corn chips, or as company with rice or other grains.

The Process

FIRST STAGE:
Any
SECOND STAGE:
Refry
BEANS:
Pinto
COOKING LIQUID:
Bean juice
SALT SEASONING:
Sea salt, tamari
OIL:
Corn oil
HERBS/SPICES:
Chili powder
VEGETABLES:
Onions, garlic, green peppers

BEANS: Any bean can be refried in this manner. To keep within the ethnic origin of this style of dish, use Anasazi, tepary, or black turtle beans.

COOKING LIQUID: The juice from the cooked beans is an important ingredient in this traditional style of refried beans. The more liquid, the looser the refried beans. Some cooks prepare beans quite wet when they accompany a grain dish. If you want a drier texture as a filling for burritos, enchiladas, or tacos, use less bean juice. Should your dish require more liquid and the beans you are using don't have enough juice, then look to beer, vegetable juice, water, or stock.

SALT SEASONING: Sea salt brings the flavors together, and tamari finishes the taste. Miso and umeboshi will work on occasion. Please use the taste and smell test.

OIL: Any oil will do, but corn and beans are traditional partners.

HERBS AND SPICES: Chili powder is optional in this dish. Usually the beans carry most of the flavor. A little garlic is standard, but otherwise anything is possible.

VEGETABLES: Onions are the only requirement. Carrots make a good alternative to green peppers, or you could combine them.

Greens and Beans and Other Things

Leafy greens with beans make my body feel strong and balanced. Based on an Italian dish of escarole or endive lightly cooked in olive oil and garlic, this dish includes beans for extra power.

Serves 4

1. Heat a heavy skillet over medium heat. Add the oil, garlic, and green onions and cook for 2 to 3 minutes. Add the escarole, salt, and garam masala, cover, and cook for 2 to 3 minutes.

2. Add the beans to the skillet next to the escarole. Combine the hickory flavoring and tamari and sprinkle over the beans. Gently mix beans in with greens. Cover and heat through about 10 minutes, stirring once or twice.

SERVING SUGGESTIONS: I ate this with rice cream as a brunch. It could also be served with plain rice or in tortillas.

2 tablespoons olive oil
1 clove garlic, minced
5 green onions, slivered
6 cups escarole, cut into squares
½ teaspoon sea salt
½ teaspoon garam masala
1½ cups cooked navy beans, drained
3 tablespoons tamari
Fraction of a teaspoon hickory flavoring (liquid smoke)

The Process

BEANS: Any bean could work with this style of dish. Black-eyed peas are especially good.
SALT SEASONING: Umeboshi or diluted miso could also work in this dish.
OIL: I used olive oil for an Italian flavor, but any oil will work.
HERBS AND SPICES: I was leaning toward tarragon, basil, oregano, or dill, but my nose couldn't keep me away from the garam masala. And then the hickory flavoring reminded me of Valerie's vegetarian Hoppin' John, a Southern dish of black-eyed peas usually made with a ham hock.
VEGETABLES: Much variety is possible here: kale or collard greens, romaine or leaf lettuce, chicory, mustard greens, or turnip or beet tops. Pick one and make it stand out. Greens cook down quite a bit, so don't use fewer than 6 to 8 cups. The onion family can be varied, with white or yellow onions, leeks, or shallots replacing the green onions.

FIRST STAGE:
Pressure-cook
SECOND STAGE:
Refry
BEANS:
Navy
COOKING LIQUID:
None
SALT SEASONING:
Sea salt, tamari
OIL:
Olive oil
HERBS/SPICES:
Ggarlic, garam masala, hickory flavoring
VEGETABLES:
Green onions, escarole

BOILING:
To combine cooked beans
with other ingredients in an
abundant supply of cooking
liquid
ENERGETICS:
Gentle, rolling, slow, steady
motion
FORM:
Soup

RULE FOR TEXTURE:
You can't overcook beans if
you have the proper liquid
ratio. It's not how long you
cook the beans; it's how much
cooking liquid you give them
to expand. Too much liquid,
too much expansion.

Boiling

Boiling brings a free, rolling, loose, and liquid quality to a dish. Most cookbooks call it soup. Soup, a grand topic by itself, offers three styles for bean cookery: one, a clear broth with a somewhat equal proportion of loose vegetables and beans floating about freely, as in minestrone; two, a puree made from a concentrated portion of beans; and three, a thick, stewlike group of beans and vegetables bound by a thickening agent, such as chili.

Boiling beans in a soup is not a rapid, high-energy situation like boiling pasta. Instead, think of a gentle, gracefully rolling energy. It's not that beans couldn't withstand a short, rapid boil; they could. But vegetables don't respond well to high-fire boiling—they turn to mush. Sometimes mush is desirable; if you are planning a blended bean soup, then the texture of the vegetables is not important. But if you choose the other style of bean soup, the clear, strong-flavored, brothy one with an abundance of loose vegetables and perhaps pasta or grain as a decorative ingredient, then rapid boiling renders most ingredients limp and bruised.

You may wonder, if you are going to boil a bean, why it can't be a first-stage method. It might make sense to you to put beans in a pot with plenty of water and just boil them until they are soft. The reason I place beans for soup or stew as a second-stage method is because the bean's integrity can be lost in a vast amount of liquid. The skins open and soon it is mush. Unless you want the beans to dissolve their shape, as in a few bean dishes like red lentil soup and split pea aspic, it is important to keep control over the texture of the beans so the intensity of flavor is not lost.

The techniques for these three variations on boiling follow. Notice the differences so that when you go to improvise, your technique is clear, offering you many more possibilities than falling into a routine bean soup.

VEGETABLE BROTH BEAN SOUP PROCEDURE

- Cut vegetables into shapes and sizes that fit into a spoon.
- Heat a heavy-bottomed soup pot. Add oil and seal each vegetable, adding one at a time at a fairly slow pace. Give the vegetables time to caramelize and brown a bit. Add herbs and spices when the vegetables are sealed.
- Lift the flavors off the bottom of the pot by adding some cooking liquid. This could be bean juice, nut milk, water, or other liquids; there usually is not enough bean juice for the entire soup, so pick another cooking liquid or two to go with it.
- Add enough salt to pull the flavors together (see Seasoning Without Measuring, page 14).
- Add the first-stage cooked beans, bring to a slow boil until all flavors become one, about 15 minutes. Adjust the salt seasoning and determine whether you will need a touch of accent liquid.

PUREED BEAN SOUP PROCEDURE

- Cook beans in a first-stage method.
- Add vegetables, herbs, spices, and salt. Sealing the vegetables first in a separate pan is optional (see Vegetable Broth Bean Soup Procedure, above). Cook until the vegetables are soft and flavors integrated.
- Blend ⅓ to ½ of the soup, leaving the rest of the beans and vegetables whole. Adjust the seasoning.

STEW-STYLE BEAN SOUP PROCEDURE

- Heat a large, heavy-bottomed pot and add oil, herbs, spices, and onions. Cook until onions are clear.
- Add the other vegetables, sealing them one at a time. It's optional to sauté the binder (corn, garbanzo, or rice flour, or millet, rice, or quinoa) with the vegetables.
- Add first-stage cooked beans, cooking liquid, and salt.
- If you didn't sauté the binder with the vegetables, mix it into the broth now. If you are using flour, make a paste in some cool liquid before adding it to the pot.
- Simmer for at least 45 minutes. Adjust seasonings.

Lentil Soup

1 tablespoon olive oil
2 cloves chopped garlic
1 cup chopped onion (1 medium)
1 cup finely diced carrots (2 medium)
½ cup finely diced parsnips (1 small)
2 cups finely diced zucchini (1 medium)
2 tablespoons dry basil
1 teaspoon fennel seed, crushed
4 cups cooked lentils, drained
10 cups water (include lentil juice, if any)
1 tablespoon vegetable salt
1 to 2 tablespoons tomato paste (optional)
1 bay leaf
1½ to 2 cups curly, elbow, or spiral noodles
¼ cup tamari, or to taste

This multivegetable soup is one of the most versatile dishes in history. It seems you can make lentil soup with almost anything. This dish can be simple with very few ingredients or complex, using many herbs and vegetables. Either way, the delightful flavor of lentils carries the soup. This recipe was made from ingredients at hand. I also like to include turnip, rutabaga, and burdock root in small quantities as additions or substitutions.

Serves 8

1. Heat a soup pot over medium heat. Add the oil, garlic, and onion sealing them until the onion is clear and somewhat brown. One at a time, add the carrots, parsnips, and zucchini, then the herbs. Take the time to slowly seal each vegetable before adding the next; this can take half an hour in all, but it's worth it.

2. Add the lentils and cooking liquid, stirring the bottom of the pot. Add the salt and bay leaf, bring to a slow boil, and cook for 10 minutes.

3. Add the noodles and simmer until the noodles have swelled and are tender. If not serving the soup right away, turn off the heat when you add the noodles; they will soften as the soup stands.

4. Adjust the seasoning with tamari.

SERVING SUGGESTIONS: This soup is nice topped with large croutons. Heat French bread slices in the oven (you may want to brush them with olive oil and garlic first) and dip the slices into the soup. Notice the contrasting textures. This soup can be either the first course to be followed by grain, sauce, and cooked and raw vegetable dishes, or the main course, supported by a salad.

The Process

BEANS: Any medium-cooking bean accommodates this style of soup.

COOKING LIQUID: I frequently use water in addition to whatever bean juice is left when the beans are cooked. You could add an interesting flavor with some sake in the cooking liquid. When using alcohol, use whatever strength you deem appropriate in combination with water or vegetable stock.

SALT SEASONING: Some sea salt is necessary to help integrate the flavors of all the ingredients, but tamari makes this loose vegetable style soup richer. You could substitute a light miso or some umeboshi vinegar, but do the taste and smell test first (page 15).

OIL: I prefer a vegetable oil for this method; it creates a better stock base from the vegetables than ghee. But any fat will do. Try to select an oil that has some character, such as hazelnut or sesame.

HERBS AND SPICES: Fresh garlic is almost a standard ingredient for bean soup. But you could replace it with shallots. Thyme and marjoram make good additions or substitutions. Sweet spices, such as fennel, cinnamon, or clove, can bring a delightful taste, particularly in combination with tomatoes. For a most unusual effect, try mint.

VEGETABLES: It's really the vegetables that make the distinction in this soup. Try combinations such as zucchini, tomatoes, and fresh fennel; rutabaga, burdock, and winter squash; or carrots, green peppers, and Jerusalem artichokes. Lentils are small, so cut vegetables into compatibly sized pieces.

FIRST STAGE:
Steep
SECOND STAGE:
Boil
BEANS:
Lentils
COOKING LIQUID:
Water, bean juice
SALT:
Vegetable salt, tamari
OIL:
Olive oil
HERBS/SPICES:
Garlic, basil, fennel, bay leaf
VEGETABLES:
Onions, carrots, parsnips, zucchini, tomato paste

White Bean Soup

1 tablespoon ghee
2 cups diced onions
8 cloves fresh garlic, chopped
1½ cups carrots, cut in ½ moon shape
½ cup celery, cut thin on a diagonal
2 cups diced potatoes
3 cups cooked navy beans, drained
5 cups combined bean juice and water
1 tablespoon pickling spices, tied in cheesecloth packet
1 teaspoon crushed red pepper (optional)
¼ cup wild rice, washed
½ cup raw almonds
1 tablespoon sea salt
½ teaspoon natural hickory flavoring (optional)
1 cup fresh parsley, chopped, for garnish

This soup has a creamy texture even without pureeing the beans. Vegetables and beans float together in a rich full-flavored stock, giving the soup a chowderlike quality. Change the vegetables to include kohlrabi and parsnips. Hot peppers are definitely optional, so if your mouth is sensitive, don't use them.

Serves 6-8

1. Heat a soup pot over medium heat. Add the ghee, onions, and garlic, cooking over medium-high heat until the onions are clear.

2. Add the carrots, celery, and potatoes and cook to seal. Take time to cook each by itself before adding the next one.

3. Add the beans, bean juice and water, red pepper, pickling spices, and wild rice. Cook at a slow boil for 30 minutes.

4. Meanwhile, make almond milk. If using a food processor, blend the almonds into a paste, then gradually add 1 cup water. If using a blender, combine the water and almonds and blend until smooth. Strain the milk through a cheesecloth, squeezing milk away from the fiber. Straining is optional.

5. Add the almond milk, salt, and hickory flavoring to the soup. Cook for 15 more minutes, then adjust the final taste. Remove the packet of pickling spices and mix in parsley just before serving.

SERVING SUGGESTIONS: Serve with sourdough or rye bread toasted with butter or olive oil and a great green salad.

The Process

BEANS: Other white beans—lima, great northern, or cannellini—maintain the color of this soup. Garbanzo beans could be used in a similar style soup with a nut milk base, but you would probably want to change some of the other elements.

COOKING LIQUID: Almond milk provides the creamy base for this soup. Beans by nature are kind of heavy-feeling, so I chose almonds because their milk is light and not too rich. Filbert (hazelnut) milk would be a good alternative, or try pecans or pistachios.

SALT SEASONING: This soup is so beautifully white, it would be a shame to discolor it, so plain sea salt is the best option. If the flavors would work, umeboshi vinegar could be used in combination with some sea salt without changing the color.

OIL: Ghee was chosen to assist the creamy white feeling of this dish. Sesame or safflower oil could substitute, but be careful of too much browning. Nut milk adds oil.

HERBS AND SPICES: I couldn't take my eyes off the pickling spices on the shelf. Determined to find a place in bean cookery for them, I think I found a pretty good one in this soup. Optional flavors could be caraway and fennel seed with a cinnamon stick.

VEGETABLES: Potatoes, carrots, and celery are everyday ingredients. To make this a more dramatic dish, replace one of these with a more exotic vegetable, such as fresh fennel in place of celery, buttercup squash in place of potato, or parsnip in place of carrot.

FIRST STAGE:
Pressure-cook
SECOND STAGE:
Boil
BEANS:
Navy
COOKING LIQUID:
Bean juice, water, nut milk
SALT SEASONING:
Sea salt
OIL:
Ghee, almonds
HERBS/SPICES:
Pickling spices, garlic, hot pepper, hickory smoke flavoring
VEGETABLES:
Onions, carrots, celery, potatoes, wild rice, parsley

Garbanzo and Carrot Soup

1 tablespoon sesame oil
2 garlic cloves, peeled
2 cups onions, coarsely cut
1 cup carrots, coarsely cut
Seeds from 3 cardamom
    pods, crushed
1½ cup cooked garbanzo
    beans, drained
3 cups water or vegetable
    stock
1¼ teaspoon sea salt

In this creamy soup, carrots are pureed along with the beans to create a smooth and colorful dish. In addition to or in place of carrots, you might try red peppers and winter squash and leave out the cardamom. The sweet red pepper variation, created by Martha Morvan during improvisation, offers an exotic, almost neon quality to the dish. You don't really have to crush the cardamom seeds; it's just that munching them whole shocks the palate.

Serves 4

1. In a heavy-bottomed soup pot or pressure cooker, sauté the garlic, onions, and carrots in the sesame oil. Add the cardamom seeds, water or stock, and sea salt. Cook until the vegetables are soft.

2. In a food processor or blender, blend the cooked garbanzo beans together with the cooked vegetables until smooth.

3. Heat and adjust the seasonings before serving.

SERVING SUGGESTIONS: This soup is best served hot, although it is tempting to serve it cold. Add some croutons for texture. This is a good first course for an elegant meal.

The Process

BEANS: Pick a full-flavored bean as an alternative. Choose one that won't interfere with the color scheme, such as cannellini beans or red lentils.

OIL: Ghee, olive oil, or hazelnut oil are good alternatives.

HERBS AND SPICES: Sometimes vegetables will have enough flavor and additional spices won't be necessary. But always use some garlic or shallots. The cardamom seed in this dish opens up the palate just as spring snow clears the air. It is fairly strong. You may prefer one of the savory herbs instead, such as basil or tarragon.

COOKING LIQUID: Water allows the flavors of the carrots and garbanzo beans to express themselves. Water also feels pure and does not detract from the candid cardamom seed.

SALT SEASONING: Plain sea salt is my choice for the same reason as choosing plain water—for its purity. A different salt seasoning would abstract the focus of the carrots and beans.

VEGETABLES: Pick a vegetable compatible in color and texture. Imagine one that will puree nicely when cooked soft; parsnips, rutabagas, turnips, and cauliflower are possibilities. My first choice would be a rich orange winter squash.

FIRST STAGE:
Pressure-cook
SECOND STAGE:
Boil, blend
BEANS:
Garbanzo
COOKING LIQUID:
Water
SALT SEASONING:
Sea salt
OIL:
Sesame oil
HERBS/SPICES:
Cardamom, garlic
VEGETABLES:
Onions, carrots

Anasazi Chili

4 tablespoons olive oil
¼ cup chopped garlic
    (approximately 6 cloves)
4 tablespoons unsalted
    chili powder
1 tablespoon *epazote*
    (optional)
1 tablespoon dried sage
1 tablespoon dried basil
1 tablespoon dried
    oregano
3 tablespoons cornmeal
2 cups naturally brewed
    light beer
4 cups whole, peeled
    tomatoes with juice
2 to 3 cups cooked
    Anasazi beans
2½ teaspoons vegetable
    salt (Spike)
2 or 3 large dried ancho
    chilies, stems and
    seeds removed
2 green peppers, diced
1 cup canned roasted
    green chilies, diced
1 cup fresh cilantro, as
    garnish
1 cup Traditional Foods
    brand barbecue seitan
    (optional)

Probably the most famous form of bean stew, chili has a great reputation to uphold in the West. There are as many recipes as there are telephone poles. When you are not cooking with meat, the success of this dish depends on the quality of ingredients. So find good chiles. This recipe is mild and has an unusual group of tastes, especially when you use *epazote*. If you are a macho chili eater when it comes to hot flavors, use crushed dried red chiles to turn up the heat.

Serves 6-8

1. Heat a large heavy-bottomed pot over medium heat. Add the olive oil and sauté the garlic, chili powder, *epazote,* sage, basil, oregano and cornmeal until the oil is well stained with the chili powder.

2. With a whisk and a quick hand, stir in the beer to make a smooth paste. Add the tomatoes and their juice, crushing the tomatoes by hand as you add them to the pot. Add the remaining ingredients except the seitan and cook for at least 1 hour. (You really need a heavy pot for this slow-boiling bean dish; use a flame tamer if you have lightweight cookware.)

3. If using seitan, chop it into small pieces in a food processor. Or deep-fry larger pieces to a crisp texture. Add to the chili about 15 minutes before serving.

SERVING SUGGESTIONS: Serve with corn bread and salsa. A dollop of sour cream or garnish of raw onion and grated cheese may complete this dish for you. But they are not necessary to enjoy this vegetarian chili.

The Process

BEANS: Kidney, pinto, and bolita beans are all good choices for this dish.

COOKING LIQUID: A good light beer takes this dish of beans into a new dimension. Red wine is also an option, but beer is best. Use the juice from the tomato can if you are using canned tomatoes as well as any juice remaining in the beans, but try not to dilute this dish with water.

SALT SEASONING: You could easily use tamari, but it just doesn't feel right when this has such a strong Latin American flavor. The beer in the cooking liquid already offers a fermented flavor.

OIL: Corn oil or ghee can replace olive oil in this dish.

HERBS AND SPICES: There are many possible alterations in this category. *Epazote* is optional and may be hard to find. It gives the dish an odd but authentic flavor. Crushed annatto seeds will give a similar taste.

VEGETABLES: This dish relies more on spices than vegetables for its character and flavor. But on occasion, I add carrots, which sweeten the spicy flavors.

FIRST STAGE:
Electric crock
SECOND STAGE:
Boil
BEANS:
Anasazi
COOKING LIQUID:
Beer, tomato juice
SALT SEASONING:
Vegetable salt
OIL:
Olive oil
HERBS/SPICES:
Garlic, *epazote*, sage, basil, oregano, ancho chilies, green chiles, cilantro, chili powder
VEGETABLES:
Green peppers

Black Bean Soup

3 cups cooked black turtle beans
7 cups water (including any bean juice)
2 cloves garlic, minced
2 cups diced onions
½ cup diced green peppers
1 cup mild green chilies, roasted, peeled, and diced
2 teaspoons sea salt
¼ cup tamari, or to taste
1 to 2 tablespoons fresh lime juice
½ cup fresh cilantro

The lovely thing about this soup is that it needs no oil and only relies on a few ingredients to bring about robust flavor. This is one time when I don't worry about boiling the vegetables; it leaches their flavor into the soup, and the dark color from the beans takes over and you don't see how limp the vegetables actually are. Linda Hubbly makes a Jamaican variation on a black bean soup by using Pick-a-Peppa sauce in place of the chilies and cilantro. Nona uses cumin.

Serves 8

1. Combine the beans, water, bean juice, garlic, onions, green peppers, chilies, and salt in a soup pot. Bring to a slow boil and cook for 20 to 30 minutes.

2. Blend half of the soup and put it back in the pot. Add tamari, lime juice, and cilantro to taste before serving.

SERVING SUGGESTIONS: Serve this soup with corn bread and marinated vegetable salad.

The Process

FIRST STAGE:
Pressure-cook
SECOND STAGE:
Boil
BEANS:
Black turtle
COOKING LIQUID:
Water, bean juice
SALT SEASONING:
Sea salt, tamari
OIL:
None
HERBS/SPICES:
Garlic, green chilies, cilantro
VEGETABLES:
Onions, green peppers

BEANS: With few ingredients, this style of soup needs a full-flavored bean. Small red, kidney, or tongue of fire beans would be good alternatives because they all have deep, rich colors and can easily hide the sorry look of boiled vegetables.

COOKING LIQUID: Black bean juice from the first-stage cooking method is totally appropriate for this soup. Water provides substance. Kahlúa (Mexican coffee liqueur) could be used as an accent liquid.

SALT SEASONING: Sea salt brings the flavor of the ingredients out to dance, and tamari adds a finishing touch.

OIL: This is one bean soup that requires no oil. Again, it is due to the fact that the vegetables don't need to look good. They actually blend and lose themselves into the darkness of the bean.

HERBS AND SPICES: Spices always help beans. Cumin is a popular choice for this dish, but I just don't like it, so you won't find it in many dishes in this book. Mild green chilies are strong enough and blend well, without overpowering the taste of the bean. You can find them roasted and peeled in cans in the Mexican or gourmet food sections of most supermarkets. The seeds and the thin membrane around the seeds are the hot part in hot peppers. Fresh cilantro makes this dish spectacular; although if cooking for anyone under the age of eighteen, you might want to reserve it as a garnish. Young people don't always care for this unusual taste. Neither do some older people.

VEGETABLES: This is a solid bean soup pureed to make a creamy background. The vegetables are in a supporting role, not competing for attention as in the White Bean Soup on page 94. The vegetables you use will influence the color of the puree slightly, so pay attention to how much carrot or squash you use if you choose them. Green pepper acts more as spice than a vegetable.

Corn Bread

This is the best recipe for corn bread I have ever found. Baked in a cast iron skillet, it comes out crisp on the outside and moist on the inside, with a strong corn flavor. The gift of this recipe is that it has no wheat or dairy at all. I usually use an egg, but that can be replaced with lecithin granules if you are willing to have a denser, more crumbly bread. Use unrefined corn oil as a first choice. Ghee or safflower oil could stand in, but there is nothing like a good corn oil in this dish.

3 cups cornmeal
3 tablespoons unrefined corn oil
1 teaspoon sea salt
2 cups boiling water
1 cup cold water
1 egg (optional)
2 teaspoons aluminum-free baking powder
Oil for skillet

Serves 6

1. Combine the cornmeal, salt, and oil by rubbing it through your hands until all the oil is evenly distributed. Mix in the hot water with a whisk, beating gently until smooth. Let this batter sit until it reaches room temperature, about 30 minutes (this step ensures a soft texture).

2. Preheat the oven to 375°F. Place a 10-inch skillet or 8 × 11-inch baking pan in the oven as it preheats.

3. Mix the cold water into the batter. Remove the baking pan from the oven and drizzle some oil into it, rolling the pan or using a brush to make the oil cover the bottom and all corners and edges.

4. Combine the egg and baking powder in a separate cup or bowl, mixing with vigor until the first part of the double action (that which rises with liquid) is engaged. Fold this foamy substance into the batter. Pour the batter into the oiled pan and bake until a toothpick inserted in the center comes out dry, 25 to 35 minutes. Invert onto a platter and serve upside down.

Red Lentil and Leek Soup

1 cup raw red lentils
7 cups water
2 inches kombu
2 cups leeks, cut small
(green and white parts)
½ cup raw cashews
2 teaspoons sea salt
1 teaspoon fresh rosemary,
minced
½ teaspoon raspberry
vinegar

I think of red lentils as similar to split peas, only lighter energetically. This is a very elegant soup, simple, creamy, light, and aromatic. Here is another case where first-stage and second-stage methods are not so clearly separate.

Serves 6–8

1. In a five-quart soup pot, boil the red lentils in 5 cups water with kombu until they are soft and almost disappear into the thick broth, about 40 minutes.

2. In a blender or food processor, make nut milk with the cashews and 2 cups water (see White Bean Soup, page 94, for the nut milk technique). Add to the soup pot with the leeks, salt, and rosemary. Stir until the heat comes to medium. Cover and simmer at least 20 minutes.

3. Add the raspberry vinegar just before serving and mix thoroughly.

SERVING SUGGESTIONS: Croutons (recipe follows) add texture and complementary grain. A marinated vegetable salad among fresh lettuce greens completes a light meal; or make the soup the first course of an elegant dinner.

The Process

FIRST STAGE:
Steep
SECOND STAGE:
Boil
BEANS:
Red lentil
COOKING LIQUID:
Cashew milk, raspberry
vinegar
SALT SEASONING:
Sea salt
OIL:
Cashews
HERBS/SPICES:
Rosemary
VEGETABLES:
Leeks

BEANS: I would try this with split peas if they weren't so hard to get soft at this altitude. Lima beans would work well, especially if you puree them after this first-stage cooking method. You see, perfectly cooked red lentils are mushy. I haven't figured out how to keep them whole and have them cooked.

COOKING LIQUID: Water, in the nut milk, is the major cooking liquid here. White wine may be substituted in small proportions while making the nut milk or for adjusting the substance of the soup. For instance, your first-stage beans may be drier than the ones I was working with in this recipe. So, to get the texture you like for a light creamy soup, a touch of wine may be just the thing. Raspberry vinegar acts as an accent liquid to help lighten the richness of the nut milk and red lentil puree. It's not enough to make the soup sour; it simply lightens it.

SALT SEASONING: Plain salt is my choice for integrating the flavors of these ingredients. It is simple and direct. Perhaps light miso would be a possibility; the color would work well in this light-colored soup, and the flavor would add a good dimension. Umeboshi could also be a successful ingredient if you eliminate the raspberry vinegar.

OIL: Oil for this dish is in the cashew milk. Other nut milks make delicious soups; pecan, filbert, and almost all would be elegant alternatives.

VEGETABLES: Only one vegetable, an onion family, is used in this very simple dish. Diced carrots, parsnips, burdock root, celery, or rutabaga could be added, but a representative of the onion family should stay. More is not necessarily better in the simple, elegant soup.

Dilled Croutons

Serves 6-8

1. Preheat the oven to 325°F. Heat a heavy-bottomed skillet. Add the oil and scallions or chives, taking a minute to seal, then add the dill and turn off the heat.

2. Toss the bread cubes in the herb-flavored oil (in the skillet if it is large enough or in a bowl, however it is easiest to get them together). Carefully press the herbs into the bread as you mix.

3. Turn the cubes out on a cookie sheet and bake until crisp and golden. Turn frequently as they bake. Remove from the oven and toss with tamari to taste.

7 pieces yeast bread, cut in cubes
4 tablespoons olive oil
½ cup minced scallions or chives
4 tablespoons minced fresh dill
Tamari to taste

Minestrone

2 tablespoons olive oil
8 cloves garlic, chopped
2 tablespoons dried basil
2 tablespoons dried oregano
1 tablespoon fennel seed, crushed
1 tablespoon dried thyme
2 cups onions, diced
1 cup carrot, split and diagonally sliced
1 cup celery, sliced
1 cup cooked kidney beans
1 cup cooked garbanzo beans
6 cups water and/or bean juice
¼ cup Marsala wine
1½ teaspoons sea salt
1 bay leaf
1½ cups spiral pasta
4 cups Swiss chard, shredded
1 teaspoon pepper
2 tablespoons tamari, or to taste

This meal in a bowl features beans along with pasta and leafy greens. Marietta Sisca teaches that tomatoes are not a standard ingredient to minestrone, contrary to popular thoughts about this Italian soup and canned versions. Condiments, such as garlic bread, croutons, or a splash of Parmesan cheese, highlight the composition.

Serves 8

1. Heat a heavy-bottomed soup pot over medium-high heat. Add the oil, onions, basil, oregano, fennel, and thyme. Add the carrots, taking time to cook them slowly. When golden, add the celery and cook for at least 5 minutes, creating a good base of flavors at the bottom of the pot.

2. Add the beans and cooking liquids. Stir and scrape to loosen the flavors from the bottom of the pot. Add the salt and bay leaf and cook at a slow boil for about 5 minutes. Add the pasta, cook for 5 minutes, then add the greens, tamari, and pepper. Simmer another 10 minutes.

SERVING SUGGESTIONS: Serve with garlic toast or French bread and a salad.

INSTANT GARLIC TOAST: Heat a skillet, add olive oil and garlic powder; lay the bread on top, brown and turn. Salt with tamari.

GARLIC BREAD: Slice a long loaf diagonally. Mix olive oil with garlic and brush on the bread slices. Wrap them together in foil or lay them individually for crispier company. Heat in the oven until nicely toasted.

The Process

BEANS: I tried to make this dish with fava beans, but they are just too foreign to my palate for me to appreciate them. But this style of bean and vegetable soup is common with almost every bean. For example, try lima beans with corn (as grain or vegetable), tomatoes, and shredded lettuce, or pinto beans with kale and green peppers.

COOKING LIQUID: Water, wine, and bean juice provide variety and dimension to a soup that is traditionally made with chicken or beef stock. Water alone will suffice in a pinch, providing you use the right amount of herbs, spices, and salt seasonings. But bean juice is always appropriate and wine, though unnecessary, makes it special.

SALT SEASONING: Sea salt and tamari share the function of salt in this dish. Sea salt extracts the multiple flavors available in the ingredients, and tamari integrates the final taste. Its fermented quality throws the final taste into a broader experience than just salt. Miso and umeboshi can shift the direction of the final taste also, but always use sea salt in the beginning, especially when water is the cooking liquid.

OIL: Olive oil carries the traditional Italian flavors. Ghee would be a good choice when inventing your own herbal and spice combinations.

HERBS AND SPICES: When water is the cooking liquid, as opposed to beef or chicken stock, herbs play a major role. Crush them through the fingers and use enough to generously speckle the vegetables. Your choice depends on your nose and taste buds. Try not to mix more than 3 to 5 or they begin to compete in a most ungraceful way. This dish has 5. Try variations, such as tarragon with lemon zest and pepper, or cilantro with garlic and paprika.

VEGETABLES: The major vegetable here is a leafy green, swiss chard. Kale, collards, escarole, romaine lettuce, and savoy cabbage fill this spot deliciously. The minor vegetables, carrot and celery, are like the two pillars of soup, and it's difficult to do without them.

FIRST STAGE:
Pressure-cook
SECOND STAGE:
Boil
BEANS:
Kidney, garbanzo
COOKING LIQUID:
Marsala wine, water, bean juice
SALT SEASONING:
Sea salt
OIL:
Olive oil
HERBS/SPICES:
Garlic, basil, oregano, fennel, thyme, bay leaf
VEGETABLES:
Onions, carrots, celery, Swiss chard

Basic Split Pea Soup

2 teaspoons sesame oil
½ cup diced onion
½ cup leeks, cut small
½ cup finely diced carrots
¼ cup finely diced celery
3 cups cooked split peas
1 to 2 cups water
1 bay leaf
**1½ teaspoons vegetable
     salt (Spike)**
**2 drops hickory flavoring
     (liquid smoke – optional)**

Onions, carrots, and celery are almost always in my refrigerator. This is a dish you could make on the spot, with no fancy ingredients required. Hickory flavoring is natural and optional.

Serves 4

1. Heat a heavy-bottomed soup pot over medium-high heat. Add the oil, onion, and leeks and cook until clear and slightly golden.

2. Add the carrots, toss them with the onions, and cook for at least 5 minutes. Do the same with the celery.

3. Add the split peas, water, bay leaf, salt, and hickory flavoring. Cook for 30 minutes at a slow boil. Adjust salt seasoning if necessary.

The Process

FIRST STAGE:
Steep
SECOND STAGE:
Boil
BEANS:
Split pea
COOKING LIQUID:
Water
SALT SEASONING:
Vegetable salt
HERBS/SPICES:
Bay leaf, hickory flavoring
VEGETABLES:
Onions, leeks, carrots, celery

BEANS: Yellow and green split peas are interchangeable. Red and yellow lentils (both of which are also split) are also possibilities.
COOKING LIQUID: Water, the simplest liquid of all, gives this soup a thinner substance than most. Add a bouillon cube if you don't use the vegetable salt. Sherry or sake in small amounts could enhance this dish, but it really needs very little fiddling.
SALT SEASONING: Vegetable salt makes this simple group of ingredients more complex tasting. You can use plain salt if you use a group of more powerful vegetables and seal them for a long time. Tamari, miso, and umeboshi also make good alternative salt seasonings; but try to use a little sea salt even with these so that the other ingredients can let their flavors loose in the cooking liquid.
OIL: Ghee, olive, sesame, or hazelnut oil are my favorites. You could avoid oil altogether, but the flavors won't mix as well and the vegetables will feel spent.
HERBS AND SPICES: Bay leaf gives a certain depth to this simple soup. Hickory flavoring provides the smoky taste of salt pork or ham that permeates most split pea soups. This natural, vegetarian version of the smoky taste is a powerful ingredient. Just a few drops should be enough.
VEGETABLES: Always use some onion family members and a root vegetable. Burdock, parsnip, or rutabaga can replace or join the carrots. Bell peppers, like celery, bring zing into the flavors; use them sparingly.

Marinating

This popular second-stage cooking method most often takes the form of a salad, either served as itself or as marinated beans used to decorate a lettuce or pasta salad. The whole success of this dish relies on three things: the integrity of the beans, the cold sauce, and the decorative vegetables.

Integrity of the beans is essential, even more than in other methods. The skin must surround the meat of the bean without a split. See pages 11–12 for more about this crucial quality in bean cookery.

Composing a cold sauce (dressing) is a fun game of mix and match. As long as you pay attention to the rules of improvisation, this cooking method can be the easiest, most enticing of all. Cold sauces are composed of cooking liquid, salt seasoning, oil, herbs and spices. Sometimes oil is an optional ingredient. Oil balances a strong accent liquid. Even a little oil provides a vehicle in which flavors travel. For example, if your cooking liquid is a sweet fruit juice, then you can use zero to very little oil to help the continuity of the dish. Light or dark sesame oil or hazelnut oil are good choices for this fruity selection. If you choose a strong accent liquid, such as vinegar or lemon juice for your cooking liquid, then more oil will be required. The actual amount of oil you use will depend on the volume of marinade that is required to cover however many beans you are using.

Decorative vegetables dramatize a marinated bean dish, adding accents of color, texture, and flavor. Black olives against white beans, or red pepper against black beans, create contrast. Avoid cabbage. It's tempting to use purple cabbage as a decorative vegetable but if anyone has the slightest digestive sensitivity, this combination could be quite disruptive.

Store marinated beans in the refrigerator. The sour taste of the marinade can be confused with the sour taste of a spoiling bean. Any slow warming of the bean marinade can accelerate this decomposition, shifting it from a pleasant sour experience to a gastronomical disaster. If you notice a tingly sensation at the top of your tongue, a sour note as opposed to a refreshing sour taste from the sides of your tongue, throw out the beans.

MARINATING:
Soaking cooked beans in a cold sauce
ENERGETICS:
Cool, bathing in an uplifting liquid
FORM:
Salad

RULES FOR IMPROVISATION:
Avoid duplicate ingredients from the same category unless they have a separate function. Use the taste and smell test to bring certainty about using an ingredient. Pay attention to color and texture. Engage your attention and intention.

PROCEDURE

- Select an oil and salt seasoning. Mix them together, beating well to a creamy consistency.
- Add herbs and spices and blend well.
- Add a sour liquid and blend well. Adjust the seasonings to your taste.
- Add decorative vegetables. Toss to coat evenly and let them soak up the flavors for 1 or 2 minutes.
- Add the cooked beans. Mix well and refrigerate for about 1 hour, stirring from time to time.

Marinated Three Beans

1 cup whole green beans
2 tablespoons olive oil
2 tablespoons wine vinegar
1 teaspoon sea salt
3 tablespoons fresh basil
1 teaspoon black pepper
½ cup cooked kidney beans
½ cup cooked garbanzo beans
¼ cup toasted tamari pumpkin seeds (no shell)

My favorite part of this dish is roasted, tamari-flavored pumpkin seeds (pepitas). They balance the heavy dose of beans with a nutty crunch. Don't put them in until serving time.

Serves 4–6

SERVING SUGGESTIONS: This is a great side dish to pasta or mixed in with pasta or lettuce salad and French or other Old World bread.

1. Heat ⅛ inch of water in a skillet over high heat. Add a pinch of sea salt and the green beans. Toss. Cover. When the water is gone and the beans are bright green and cooked evenly, stop the cooking by dropping the beans in cold water. Drain and cut into slivers.

2. Mix the oil, vinegar and sea salt, basil, and pepper in a large enough bowl to hold all the ingredients. Add the kidney, garbanzo, and green beans. Toss to coat. Let sit for 2 hours, tossing at regular intervals.

3. Sprinkle with pumpkin seeds at serving.

The Process

BEANS: Other beans can also work beautifully in this method, as long as they have integrity. Notice how the other recipes in this section all work the same way. Go ahead and marinate black–eyed peas, lima beans, pintos, or azuki beans.

COOKING LIQUID: Vinegar is the featured cooking liquid in this process. If you prefer a sweet taste, you might rely on mirin or orange juice, or make honey water (honey diluted in warm water).

SALT SEASONING: Plain sea salt integrates the flavors most directly, but miso, tamari, and umeboshi vinegar can be used when coordinated with the other ingredients.

OIL: Choose an oil that has some character. Hazelnut oil would be delicious.

HERBS AND SPICES: These can be complex or simple. Try tarragon or arugula as individual options, or pickling spices as a complex group of tastes.

VEGETABLES: Green beans are considered a vegetable. Additional vegetables would detract from the three-bean emphasis, although jicama, radishes, green onions, celery, olives, and peppers can be decorative additions.

FIRST STAGE:
Pressure-cook
SECOND STAGE:
Marinate
BEANS:
Garbanzo, kidney
COOKING LIQUID:
Wine vinegar
SALT SEASONING:
Sea salt
OIL:
Olive oil, pumpkin seeds
HERBS/SPICES:
Basil, pepper
VEGETABLES:
Green beans

Mung Bean Sprouts and Green Beans With Candied Walnuts

¼ cup mirin
3 tablespoons white rice vinegar
½ teaspoon sea salt
1 teaspoon fresh ginger juice (grate about 1 inch fresh ginger, squeeze to extract juice)
2 green onions, slivered very thin diagonally
2 cups fresh green beans, steeped or blanched, cut thin on a long diagonal
5 cups fresh mung bean sprouts
1 cup candied walnuts (see below – optional)

FIRST STAGE:
Sprout
SECOND STAGE:
Marinate
BEANS:
Mung
COOKING LIQUID:
Mirin, rice vinegar
SALT SEASONING:
Sea salt
OIL:
Walnuts (optional)
HERBS/SPICES:
Ginger
VEGETABLES:
Green onions, green beans

If you leave out the walnuts, there is no oil in this dish. It is clear and refreshing. The marinade invites you to devour the vegetables. Look at the process to inspire variety in this dish.

Serves 4

1. Mix the mirin, vinegar, salt, and ginger juice.

2. Sprinkle a small amount of sea salt on the green onions and press them slightly.

3. Toss the green onions, green beans, mung sprouts, and walnuts in the marinade about 5 minutes before serving time.

SERVING SUGGESTIONS: Serve chilled or at room temperature with a creamy soup and a cooked grain dish.

The Process

BEANS: It's the long watery tail of this bean sprout that is so delicious and edible. The soybean (in the form of sprouts) is the only other bean that I know of that could perform in this dish. But the soybeans would have to be steamed first, and then they would be too limp to be crispy.
COOKING LIQUID: Mirin provides the base for the marinade, while rice vinegar provides the accent. Orange juice could replace mirin, and lime juice or apple cider vinegar can replace rice vinegar.
SALT SEASONING: Tamari could be used in combination with sea salt but it would change the color. This may be just the look you want. Miso can work, but the marinade will appear somewhat cloudy.
OIL: This dish can easily be served without any oil; just eliminate the walnuts. For a striking look, you can also replace the candied walnuts with toasted, slightly crushed black sesame seeds.
HERBS AND SPICES: Fresh ginger brings about a delicious warmth. Cilantro or arugula would be a good addition.
VEGETABLES: I have chosen lightweight, watery vegetables for this dish. Radishes, cucumbers, fresh green peas or pea pods, shiitake mushrooms, bamboo shoots, baby corn, celery, or water chestnuts make good lightweight additions or alternatives. If adding carrots, broccoli, or asparagus, steep or steam them first.

Candied Walnuts

1. Preheat the oven to 325°F. Bake the nuts on a sheet pan until they are just roasted, but not too dark, 10 to 12 minutes.

2. Combine the barley malt and rice syrup in a heavy-bottomed sauce pan and bring to a boil. Cook for 3 minutes, stirring the entire time. When you lift the spoon out of the pan, the ribbon should hold its form as you count to 2.

3. Add the salt, sucanat, and cinnamon, mix well, and pour over the nuts. Coat them thoroughly and set them in a separate bowl to cool.

SERVING SUGGESTIONS: Use as a garnish in salads, on grain, or as a snack.

1 cup walnut halves
1 tablespoon barley malt
1 tablespoon rice syrup
1 tablespoon sucanat
   (natural brown sugar)
¼ teaspoon sea salt
¼ teaspoon cinnamon
   (optional)

Tongue of Fire Vinaigrette

4 tablespoons extra virgin
  olive oil
1 clove garlic, crushed or
  pressed
1 teaspoon dried oregano
2 teaspoons dried basil
1 teaspoon sea salt
4 tablespoons sherry wine
  vinegar
½ cup thinly sliced red
  onion
½ cup red pepper, sliced
  diagonally
½ cup green onions,
  sliced diagonally
2 cups cooked tongue of
  fire beans, drained

Against bright red peppers and translucent red onions the voluptuously shaped, deep purple tongue of fire bean makes this dish look like a Renaissance painting. A slightly smoky look and flavor add to the mystique of this elegant broad bean.

Serves 6-8

1. Mix oil and garlic, pressing the garlic into the oil.

2. Crush the herbs through your fingers into the oil. Mix in the sea salt. Add the vinegar and mix well.

3. Toss the red onion, red pepper, and green onions into the marinade first, then lightly toss in the beans until they are well coated.

4. Cover and refrigerate at least one hour.

SERVING SUGGESTIONS: This is a great sandwich filling for truly crusty French bread. Slice the bread the long way. Line it with a bit of extra virgin olive oil, and lay some tongue of fire marinade in the center. Enjoy with a hearty vegetable or a creamy vegetable soup.

The Process

BEANS: I chose the tongue of fire variety for this cooking method because I wanted its large, beautiful form to stand out in a singular fashion and not be disguised as a pâté, spread, or dip. When any bean is cooked to perfection and has a body as beautiful as tongue of fire, marinating is the perfect method to show it off. Black beans, great northern, and garbanzos are a few that you will see again in this cooking method.

COOKING LIQUID: Sherry wine vinegar is the accent liquid in this dish. If you should slip and put in too much, reserve the bean juice from the first stage to soften the intensity. Other accent liquids that work for this dish are apple cider, balsamic, and rice vinegars, or lemon or lime juice.

SALT SEASONING: Sea salt, diluted in the mixing procedure with oil and vinegar, helps to make the flavors harmonious. I like plain sea salt in herbal marinades because it is neutral and allows the other ingredients to come forward. If you decide to change the salt seasoning to, let's say, tamari, then it will add a new dimension and probably be delicious as long as the color does not interfere with your intended design.

OIL: Extra virgin olive oil helps smooth out the grainy character of tongue of fire beans. If you change the oil, you might as well change everything else. Pay attention to the flavors. Should you use dark sesame oil?

VEGETABLES: Three decorative vegetables make a good design against the giant bean. Red peppers and red onions offer shades of red and purple and the green onions gives a splash of green. Parsley would also be good, chopped fine and mixed in or used as a garnish. Yellow sweet peppers could replace the red, but I would keep the red onions. There is something romantic about the soft color mimicking the deep purple bean.

HERBS AND SPICES: Oregano and basil are long-standing friends. They go most places together. If one is absent, just double the amount of the one that you have. Fresh herbs place this dish into another category of elegance; use 3 times the amount if you use fresh herbs. For alternate herbs, look into tarragon or thyme. To change this to a spicy dish, consider hot flavors like jalapeño peppers and garlic with cilantro, or fresh ginger juice and black pepper.

PRETREATMENT:
Soak, boil
FIRST STAGE:
Pressure-cook
SECOND STAGE:
Marinate
BEANS:
Tongue of fire
COOKING LIQUID:
Wine vinegar
SALT SEASONING:
Sea salt
OIL:
Olive oil
HERBS/SPICES:
Garlic, oregano, basil
VEGETABLES:
Red onions, red peppers, green onions

Black Bean Salsa Salad

3 tablespoons light
   sesame oil
1 clove garlic
1½ teaspoons sea salt
½ teaspoon black pepper
5 tablespoons raspberry
   vinegar
1 cup cilantro, coarsely
   cut (about 1 bunch)
1 cup cherry tomatoes,
   quartered
½ cup green pepper, diced
1 cup English cucumber,
   diced
½ cup fresh corn kernels
   (about one ear)
1½ cups cooked black
   beans (1 can Eden
   black beans)

I found this dish in the natural food Co-op of Nederland, Colorado. Searching for a snack after hiking, we tasted a sample of this dish. Immediately I knew that the people who made this dish did not follow a recipe. There was a kind of aliveness and intention in each bite. It was delightful to find a well-cooked bean in such a luscious marinade with abundant summer vegetables. I think they used lime juice where I chose raspberry vinegar, but this is my recollection of their creation. If you allow the bean juice from a can of Eden black beans to be part of this dish, it makes a wonderful salsa dip for sturdy corn chips.

Serves 4–6

In a large bowl, press the garlic into the oil. Add the black pepper and vinegar and whip thoroughly for about 1 minute. Add the cilantro, salt, tomatoes, green pepper, cucumbers, corn, and black beans and mix carefully until the marinade touches each piece. Let it sit at least 1 hour.

SERVING SUGGESTIONS: Serve as a dip for chips, on top of a lettuce salad, or rolled into tortillas; or simply eat it as a salad in a meal with enchiladas and guacamole.

The Process

FIRST STAGE:
Electric crock
SECOND STAGE:
Marinate
BEANS:
Black turtle
COOKING LIQUID:
Raspberry vinegar
SALT SEASONING:
Sea salt
OIL:
Light sesame oil
HERBS/SPICES:
Cilantro, garlic
VEGETABLES:
Tomatoes, green peppers,
cucumber, corn

BEANS: Any whole bean will work. Don't try this with split peas.
COOKING LIQUID: Raspberry vinegar is light and fruity, but any vinegar will work in its place. I especially like the strong contrast of balsamic vinegar or the neutral character of rice vinegar. Lime juice is also a great option.
SALT SEASONING: Sea salt performs most clearly. I like it the best because there are many other ingredients that want to add their flavor. Salt allows them to do this without being distracted by a more flavorful salt seasoning.
OIL: Sesame oil is easily replaced with olive oil. I only used the sesame because I sometimes rely on olive oil too heavily and I don't want to take advantage of it.
HERBS AND SPICES: Garlic and cilantro are the dynamic duo in this dish. Cilantro can be replaced with Italian parsley, basil, or arugula.
VEGETABLES: Your vegetable selection will depend on how you use this dish. As a salsa or salad, the summery, watery vegetables are

suitable. As a side dish, you could incorporate cooked carrots or winter squash. The sum total of decorative vegetables in this dish creates a major vegetable influence. You could have a major vegetable and just one or two decorative vegetables.

Lima Beans and Fresh Fennel in Black Currant Vinaigrette

Fresh fennel (or anise as it is sometimes labeled) acts like celery in a dish, but it has a delightfully intense licorice taste. The white bulb-shaped base is used as a vegetable, and the fern-like leaves are used as an herb.

Serves 4

Mix the vinegar, oil, pepper, and salt together, beating well until salt is dissolved. Add the beans, tomatoes, and fennel, mixing carefully after each one. Chill for at least 2 hours for the best taste.

SERVING SUGGESTIONS: Serve within a lettuce salad or next to a grain dish.

4 tablespoons black currant vinegar
2 tablespoons peanut oil
½ teaspoon black pepper
½ teaspoon sea salt
2 cups cooked lima beans, drained
1 cup quartered cherry tomatoes
1 cup sliced fresh fennel bulb and stem
¼ cup fresh fennel leaves, chopped
¼ cup fresh parsley, minced

The Process

BEANS: Almost any bean will do.
COOKING LIQUID: Raspberry vinegar is similar to black currant. Infused wine vinegars (basil and garlic) or a light-colored wine vinegar can be substituted. The deeper the flavor the better.
SALT SEASONING: Sea salt integrates the flavors with little interruption. There are no substitutes.
OIL: Peanut oil gives a strong nutty taste. Make sure it is the kind of peanut oil that has a full taste of peanuts. Olive, hazelnut, or sesame oil would be good substitutes.
HERBS AND SPICES: I like how black pepper decorates this dish and lifts the taste. Fresh fennel leaves or dill weed act as an herb and can be substituted with fresh basil or mint.
VEGETABLES: Parsley acts more as a decorative vegetable along with tomatoes. Black olives would also be an attractive addition to this red, white, and green dish.

FIRST STAGE:
Electric crock
SECOND STAGE:
Marinate
BEANS:
Lima
COOKING LIQUID:
Black currant vinegar
SALT SEASONING:
Sea salt
OIL:
Peanut oil
HERBS/SPICES:
Black pepper, parsley, fennel
VEGETABLES:
Tomatoes, fennel

Marinated Azuki Beans and Summer Squash

2 tablespoons lime juice
2 tablespoons olive oil
½ teaspoon sea salt
½ cup arugula, slivered
¾ cup steamed or steeped yellow patty pan summer squash (about 1 medium), sliced
½ cup roasted red peppers
¾ cup azuki beans
½ cup toasted, umeboshi sunflower seeds

The colors in this dish are stunning. Make sure the summer squash is perfectly cooked – not too hard, not too soft. And save the sunflower seeds for a garnish on top so that they don't become soggy.

Serves 4

1. In a large bowl, mix the lime juice, olive oil, and sea salt. Beat thoroughly and add arugula, peppers, squash, and beans. Let sit for at least 1 hour.

2. Garnish with sunflower seeds before serving.

SERVING SUGGESTIONS: Serve as a salad with cream of broccoli soup and a grain dish with a sauce.

TO ROAST PEPPERS: Wash whole peppers and place under the broiler. Broil, turning the peppers so the fire reaches all sides, until the skins are black. Wrap in a paper or plastic bag for about 30 minutes. The skin will steam itself off. Peel the peppers, keeping them as whole as possible. Juice will run out of the peppers; capture it in a bowl.

TO ROAST SUNFLOWER SEEDS: Heat a heavy-bottomed skillet over medium-high heat. Put shelled sunflower seeds into the hot skillet and stir or shake the pan to move them around evenly. They turn a deeper color as the oil in the seeds surfaces. Turn off the heat and sprinkle 1 tablespoon of umeboshi vinegar for each cup of seeds around the hot seeds, stirring constantly. Let cool, then store in an airtight glass jar if they don't get eaten in two days.

The Process

BEANS: Any whole bean can be substituted. Eden canned azukis work well in this dish.

COOKING LIQUID: Lime juice can be replaced with any vinegar or lemon juice. Azuki beans would also respond well to a sweet marinade of orange juice and mirin.

SALT SEASONING: Light miso in combination with sea salt would be a good option in place of sea salt. Tamari would ruin the color scheme.

OIL: Any oil will provide the function of taking the flavors all around the dish. Extra virgin olive oil makes a distinct, sophisticated contribution. Light sesame, safflower, or canola oil would be acceptable.

HERBS AND SPICES: Arugula is quite expressive, with a hot, pungent, somewhat bitter character. Watercress could replace it. And, of course, any fresh herb you love will work in its place.

VEGETABLES: The major vegetables, yellow summer squash and roasted red pepper, were chosen for their brilliant color and texture. When replacing them, consider color. Plan on precooking vegetables like broccoli, beets, or carrots.

FIRST STAGE:
Electric crock
SECOND STAGE:
Marinate
BEANS:
Azuki
COOKING LIQUID:
Lime juice
SALT SEASONING:
Sea salt
OIL:
Olive oil, toasted umeboshi sunflower seeds
HERBS/SPICES:
Arugula
VEGETABLES:
Yellow summer squash, roasted red peppers

Marinated French Green Lentils

1 tablespoon garlic
3 tablespoons olive oil
¼ cup lime juice
1 teaspoon sea salt
½ cup fresh cilantro, minced
1 cup English cucumber, diced small
½ cup cherry tomatoes, cut in quarters (about 6)
¼ cup black Greek olives, pitted and diced (about 5)
½ cup jicama, diced small (optional)
2 cups cooked French green lentils, drained

It's important to use French green lentils. They are quite small but burst with flavor and hold their shape well for a marinade. These flavors were brought together by Margie Klemp during Shelly's improvisation class. Jicama emphasizes the refreshing Mexican design of the ingredients.

Serves 4

1. Mix the garlic and olive oil in a large bowl, pressing the garlic with a fork into the oil and against the bowl. Add the lime juice and sea salt and beat well.

2. Combine cilantro, cucumber, tomatoes, olives, and jicama. Toss in the marinade. Mix the lentils into the vegetables. Cover and refrigerate for at least an hour for the flavors to integrate.

SERVING SUGGESTION: There are enough vegetables in this dish to make this the salad of your meal. Serve with hot grain or bread and a cooked vegetable dish.

The Process

FIRST STAGE:
Steep
SECOND STAGE:
Marinate
BEANS:
French lentils
COOKING LIQUID:
Lime juice
SALT SEASONING:
Sea salt, olives, umeboshi vinegar
OIL:
Olives and olive oil
HERBS/SPICES:
Cilantro, garlic
VEGETABLES:
Cucumber, tomatoes, olives, jicama

BEANS: Any other bean suitable for the marinade method (which rules out red lentils, split peas, and other split varieties) would work in this group of ingredients.

COOKING LIQUID: Lime juice makes this dish particularly refreshing. Lemon juice or a light vinegar would also be good.

SALT SEASONING: Sea salt brings the flavors together while umeboshi helps the watery vegetables become more than just another raw vegetable in a salad.

OIL: Olive oil can easily be replaced with peanut, safflower, canola, or light sesame.

HERBS AND SPICES: Garlic and cilantro are perfect companions. But what doesn't go with garlic? Try a different dominant herb such as rosemary for another twist.

VEGETABLES: Decorative vegetables in abundance make this dish look like a vegetable salad with lentils as the decoration. I chose watery, refreshing vegetables for this dish, but it can also work with root vegetables if they have been cooked first.

Blending

Spreads, dips, and sauces relate to each other like sisters. Sauce is the thin one, full of fire; spread is the fat one and is quite cool; and the third is in between. All three are made from the same ingredients with similar cooking methods; only the amount of cooking liquid defines the characteristic differences among them.

Beans change color in these methods, as the inside blends with the color of the outside, making the tone lighter. For example, black bean dishes become purple-grey and red bean dishes appear pink. Salt seasoning can also influence the color of your dish. Tamari deepens the natural tones, and miso, depending on the kind you use, influences the shade toward a golden to dark brown.

SPREADS AND DIPS

A spread requires no major cooking liquid. In fact, simply lifting beans away from their juice and straining them gives the perfect consistency for a spread. Modest amounts of accent liquid, salt seasoning, and oil are essential. Herbs and spices are most likely, and decorative vegetables are optional. The technique is completed by mixing or blending, with no fire required. Spreads are best as filling for bread or tortillas, or as a topping for grain croquettes.

Also made without any fire, dips use the same ingredients as spreads, but include more liquid, either accent liquid or bean juice. Dips are best served with a vegetable platter or chips.

PROCEDURE

- Blend all ingredients together; adjusting the salt seasoning to taste.
- Refrigerate to store.

SAUCES

Sauces need fire and they use a major cooking liquid. In all other respects, they are prepared like spreads and dips but they are heated to integrate the flavors. Bean sauces work well on whole grain dishes, cornbread, and steamed vegetables, and they are easily made without oil. Notice how the recipes that demonstrate this style of dish all work with the same ratio of oil to beans to cooking liquid; only the ingredients change.

BLENDING:
To mix first-stage cooked beans into a smooth consistency with a salt seasoning and the option of other ingredients
ENERGETICS:
Swift and smooth
FORM:
Spread, dips, and sauces

PROCEDURE

- Heat skillet over medium-high temperature.
- Blend cooked beans, salt seasonings, herbs, spices, and a portion of the major cooking liquid. Cook in the skillet for 10 minutes.
- Adjust substance with additional cooking liquid or fire.
- Adjust sweetness with salt seasoning or natural sweetener, such as rice or barley malt.
- Mix in the cooking liquid, blending to a smooth, not too thick consistency. It will thicken with time over the fire.
- Add decorative vegetables. Cook for at least 2 minutes. (You may sauté decorative vegetables in a small amount of oil before adding the cooked, blended beans.)

Hot Pepper Hummus

1 or 2 cloves garlic
2 cups perfectly cooked garbanzo beans, drained
3 tablespoons raw sesame tahini
½ teaspoon salt
3 tablespoons lemon juice
3 tablespoons umeboshi vinegar
½ teaspoon red pepper flakes (optional)

A really good hummus offers an even blend of tastes from sesame, garbanzo, garlic, and lemon. When these ingredients are balanced, the dish makes you sing with pleasure. This particular recipe is quite tangy and hot peppers were added on a whim. Hummus can be quite successful without them.

Yield: 2 cups

Chop the garlic in a food processor, add the beans, tahini, salt, lemon juice, umeboshi vinegar, and hot pepper flakes. Blend completely to a smooth paste. Refrigerate for at least one hour.

SERVING SUGGESTIONS: Serve on bread (pita, old country, French) with marinated vegetables, tomatoes, sprouts, olives, and lettuce. This is particularly delicious on an open-face sandwich with marinated beets.

The Process

BEANS: Other beans can follow this technique, but don't call it hummus. Most other beans change color drastically but provide a good base for dips and spreads.

COOKING LIQUID: Accent liquid helps lighten the intensity of a pureed bean. I usually look to lemon or lime, but vinegars will also work. Just use much less if you are choosing a vinegar.

SALT SEASONING: Umeboshi vinegar was chosen to assist the accent liquid. Plain sea salt can be used either in place of or in combination with umeboshi vinegar if you don't care for as much of a kick as I do. Miso and tamari are not as salty as umeboshi vinegar, so they will need some sea salt as well.

OIL: Some people add olive oil to this dish. I don't like to confuse the categories by having more than one ingredient represented. So I stay with tahini as the only oil.

HERBS AND SPICES: Garlic is an important ingredient in this traditional dish. How much you use is really optional. If you let the spread sit a while (refrigerated) before eating, the garlic taste will even out and become stronger. If you don't like garlic, use less. This particular recipe includes hot pepper flakes, which add a fantastic dimension.

VEGETABLES: On occasion I make this dish with decorative vegetables, such as green onions or parsley.

FIRST STAGE:
Pressure-cook
SECOND STAGE:
Spread
BEANS:
Garbanzo
COOKING LIQUID:
Lemon juice
SALT SEASONING:
Sea salt, umeboshi vinegar
OIL:
Sesame tahini
HERBS/SPICES:
Garlic, hot pepper
VEGETABLES:
None

Kidney Bean Dip for Artichokes

1 teaspoon minced garlic
¼ cup cooked kidney
   beans, drained (reserve
   juice)
1 tablespoon almond
   butter
¼ cup bean juice
1 tablespoon umeboshi
   vinegar

This dip was invented for an artichoke appetizer. Its soft pink color and tangy taste enhance the light green vegetable.

Yield: Enough for 2 artichokes

Blend the ingredients together into a smooth, soft dip. Let sit for 1 hour if you have time. Refrigerate.

SERVING SUGGESTIONS: Use as a dip for steamed artichokes or asparagus, or as a dressing for a salad with avocado and arugula.

The Process

FIRST STAGE:
Pressure-cook
SECOND STAGE:
Dip
BEANS:
Kidney
COOKING LIQUID:
Bean juice
SALT SEASONING:
Umeboshi vinegar
OIL:
Almond butter
HERBS/SPICES:
None
VEGETABLES:
None

BEANS: Small red beans or cranberry beans make good alternates to the larger kidney bean. They may be drier because they are smaller, so you might need a little extra bean juice.

COOKING LIQUID: Bean juice thins down the bean to a lovely puree. If you don't have any, consider using more beans and water rather than confusing the taste with another ingredient.

SALT SEASONING: Umeboshi vinegar provides three functions in this dip: it balances the oil, lightens the bean, and integrates the flavors of all the ingredients.

OIL: Almond butter is oil. Cashew, pecan, and filbert butters are all great alternate possibilities.

HERBS AND SPICES: Garlic manages this dip singlehandedly. Alternate tastes include shallot, fennel, and/or basil.

VEGETABLES: None. Decorative vegetables could be added, such as green or black olive pieces, minced green onion, parsley, or cherry tomato pieces. But this dish is designed to go with vegetables.

Pinto Bean and Olive Paste

I think of this bean dish as I think of pesto. It is rich, dynamic, delicious, and a bit decadent. Mix this deep reddish brown paste into hot pasta as a main dish, or spread it over a hot tortilla as a snack or hors d'oeuvre.

Serves 2

1. Soak the dried tomatoes in boiling water for 10 minutes. Drain.

2. In food processor, blend the garlic, olive oil, and olives to make a paste. Add the soaked tomatoes, pinto beans, and red pepper flakes. Blend to a paste. Add lime juice.

SERVING SUGGESTIONS: As a sauce for hot pasta, serve with vegetable soup and a salad.

¼ cup boiling water
½ cup dried tomatoes
6 tablespoons extra virgin olive oil
1 garlic clove sliced
¼ cup pitted oil-cured black olives (about 12)
½ cup cooked pinto beans, drained
½ teaspoon red pepper flakes
1 tablespoon lime juice

The Process

BEANS: Other reddish, pink, white, or even black beans will work beautifully. Tongue of fire, red kidney, even great northern beans will taste all right, but their color will be lighter.
COOKING LIQUID: None.
SALT SEASONING: Olives provide salt for this dish. This is a major ingredient. Change only the kind of olive you use.
OIL: The olives offer oil in addition to the extra virgin olive oil. It is conceivable to use canola oil. Sesame or hazelnut oil would fight with the olives.
HERBS AND SPICES: Garlic can be as strong as you like in this dish, as its flavor moves through pasta quite easily. Hot pepper is not too strong. Adapt the taste to your palate. Basil, tarragon, or oregano may be choices, especially if you have fresh herbs available.
VEGETABLES: Sun-dried tomatoes provide a chewy texture that when softened and pureed makes a great companion with beans. Olives have a similar quality. Together, bound by the beans, they hold the attention of this dish. There are no replacements.

FIRST STAGE:
Pressure-cook
SECOND STAGE:
Spread
BEANS:
Pinto
COOKING LIQUID:
None
SALT SEASONING:
Olives
OIL:
Olives, olive oil
HERBS/SPICES:
Garlic, red pepper flakes
VEGETABLES:
Dried tomatoes

Black Bean Cilantro Sauce

This is an elegant bean sauce. The flavors meet in an exceptional place. It's called yum.

Yield: 1½ cups

1 teaspoon olive oil
1 teaspoon chopped garlic
½ cup leeks, cut small
⅓ cup green pepper, cut small
½ cup fresh cilantro, finely cut
1 cup cooked black beans, drained
¼ cup mirin
¼ cup water
2 tablespoons tamari or shoyu
1 teaspoon blackberry vinegar

1. Heat a skillet or saucepan over medium-high heat. Add oil and garlic. One at a time, add the leeks, green pepper, and cilantro, taking time to seal each one before adding the next.

2. Blend the beans, mirin, and water to a thin consistency in a blender or food processor. Add to the vegetables and herbs in the skillet. Cook for 2 to 5 minutes.

3. Add the tamari or shoyu and vinegar and cook another until the flavors and substance are where you like them. Do not cook too long or the sauce will thicken.

SERVING SUGGESTIONS: Serve hot over corn bread or freshly cooked grain, as a sauce in *huevos rancheros,* or as company for corn chips or freshly cooked vegetables.

The Process

FIRST STAGE:
Pressure-cook
SECOND STAGE:
Sauce
BEANS:
Black turtle
OIL:
Olive oil
SALT SEASONING:
Tamari/shoyu
COOKING LIQUID:
Blackberry vinegar, lime, mirin, water
HERBS/SPICES:
Garlic, cilantro
VEGETABLES:
Leeks, green peppers

BEANS: Garbanzo beans can be substituted.

OIL: Any oil will do in this dish, but be aware of its flavor to see if it will be compatible with the other ingredients. For example, dark sesame oil would not work, but corn oil would.

SALT SEASONING: Tamari or shoyu is the only salt seasoning. If you change the bean to a lighter color, umeboshi vinegar would be a possibility.

COOKING LIQUID: The accent liquids, blackberry vinegar and lime juice, could be replaced with raspberry vinegar and lemon juice. Mirin can be replaced with sake.

HERBS AND SPICES: Garlic and cilantro are hard to beat, but they could be replaced with shallot and basil.

VEGETABLES: Leeks and green pepper add flavor and texture. Onions and red peppers make an easy alternative without changing the dish in any major way.

Kidney Bean and Roasted Pepper Sauce

The color of this dish was the inspiration. Red beans with red peppers produce a subtle glow. I could see this sauce as part of a traditional egg and tortilla dish, *huevos rancheros.*

Yield: 1½ cups

1. Heat a skillet or saucepan over medium-high heat. Add the oil, shallot, and ¼ of the roasted diced red pepper.

2. In a blender or food processor, blend the remaining red pepper, beans, salt, beer, and water. Add this mixture to the hot pan and cook for 5 minutes or until flavors have integrated and the substance is just right for a sauce.

3. Before serving, add a touch of lime juice or serve with lime wedges.

SERVING SUGGESTIONS: Serve hot over grain, over cooked vegetables such as cauliflower or squash, or over corn of any kind – chips, bread, or filled tortillas.

1 teaspoon unrefined corn oil
1 large shallot, diced (¼ cup)
1 large sweet red pepper, roasted and diced
1 cup cooked kidney beans, drained
1 teaspoon sea salt
½ cup light beer
½ cup water
1 teaspoon lime juice, or to taste

The Process

BEANS: Any bean will work in this dish. Play with the color of roasted red peppers blended with a white bean.

OIL: Unrefined corn oil is perfect with the kidney beans. Other oils will also work; balance their flavor with the other ingredients.

SALT SEASONING: Sea salt could be replaced with vegetable salt. In addition to either, a touch of tamari or umeboshi vinegar could be delicious.

COOKING LIQUID: Light beer is optional in this dish, but it brings a slightly bitter taste that goes well with the roasted peppers. You could make it simply with water and a touch of lime juice. Taste for adjusting the other seasonings when you are just using water.

VEGETABLES: This sauce was designed around the glorious taste of roasted sweet red pepper. Options for substitutions would be roasted chili peppers or roasted green pepper. Pay attention to the color scheme.

FIRST STAGE:
Pressure-cook
SECOND STAGE:
Sauce
BEANS:
Kidney
OIL:
Corn oil
SALT SEASONING:
Sea salt
COOKING LIQUID:
Beer, water, lime juice
HERBS/SPICES:
Shallot
VEGETABLES:
Roasted red peppers

White Bean and Basil Sauce

1 teaspoon olive oil
½ cup green onions
1 tablespoon fresh garlic
1 cup cooked navy beans,
    drained
¼ cup sake
¼ cup water
½ teaspoon sea salt
1 cup fresh basil, cut
    small

You might get away with serving this sauce, reminiscent of pesto, with pasta as well as grain dishes.

Yield: 1½ cups

1. Heat a skillet or saucepan over medium-high heat. Add oil and green onions and cook until sealed.

2. Combine the beans, garlic, sake, water, and salt in a food processor or blender and blend to a smooth sauce. Add to the skillet. Add the basil and cook for 5 minutes, or until the flavors meet and become one.

SERVING SUGGESTIONS: Use as a binder in casseroles or as a sauce for light grains, such as quinoa or buckwheat, or on pasta of any shape.

The Process

FIRST STAGE:
Pressure-cook
SECOND STAGE:
Sauce
BEANS:
Navy
OIL:
Olive oil
SALT SEASONING:
Sea salt
COOKING LIQUID:
Water, sake
HERBS/SPICES:
Garlic, basil
VEGETABLES:
Green onions

BEANS: Any white bean should work in place of navy beans. Great northern, cannellini, and even lima beans should work. Red and black beans will also make a good sauce, but the color will certainly be different.

OIL: Olive oil was chosen to go with the basil, but light sesame or canola would also work. But neither would be quite as satisfying as a good olive oil in this dish.

SALT SEASONING: Plain sea salt could be replaced with vegetable salt. Tamari would taint the white and green color scheme, so if you have to add a liquid salt seasoning, umeboshi may be the choice.

COOKING LIQUID: A white wine could replace the sake. If you use a red bean, try a good Merlot as the cooking liquid.

HERBS AND SPICES: Garlic helps any bean dish, and garlic and basil are practically married in the culinary world. Shallot could replace the garlic, if you use enough of it. Dill or tarragon could replace the basil.

VEGETABLES: Green onions play a modest role in this dish. You could probably eliminate them altogether. Other decorative vegetables could take part, such as red peppers or black olives.

Part III
Tofu and Tempeh Cookery

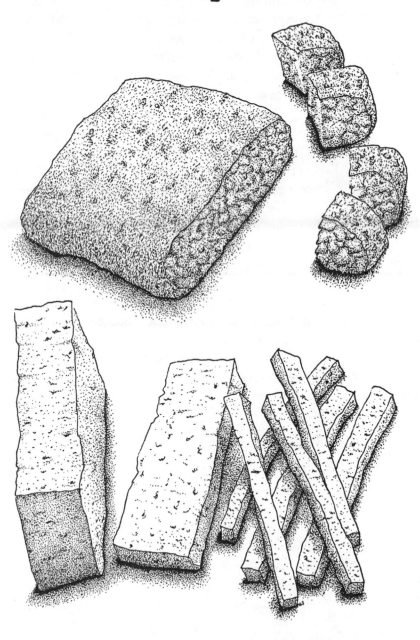

Soybeans can be cooked like other dried beans (see page 25), but in eastern Asia, where they are the most important source of protein for millions of people, they are mostly eaten in a transformed state, as tempeh or tofu. Tofu, or bean curd, is a staple in China and Japan, while tempeh, its relative, lives south of the equator in Indonesia. Ultimately, these bean products are fast food. Born from the mighty soybean, which itself is a long-cooking bean, tofu and tempeh are processed enough to eliminate the need for a long cooking time. Their manufacturing process renders their secondary compounds powerless, yielding their protein in a quickly cooked, digestible form. These products of the soybean lend themselves to the creative process equally well as whole beans. They might require pretreatments, but mostly they are worked into first-stage dishes.

Tempeh, a cake of fermented whole soybeans, contains the energetics of the whole bean, thereby offering a much more complete nutritional scope than tofu. Tempeh contains more than twice the percent of protein by weight as tofu. When either one is combined with whole grains, the usable protein is greatly increased. Soy foods are also known for their polyunsaturated fats (linoleic and linoleic acids) and lecithin content, which thin out and help eliminate excess cholesterol and fatty deposits. Among other vitamins and minerals, including a generous amount of calcium, iron, and phosphorus, tempeh retains the highest source of vegetarian B12, and it is not destroyed during cooking. It even offers an antibiotic effect similar to the effect that penicillin mold has in helping us resist infection. (See Shurtleff & Aoyagi, *The Book of Tempeh,* Chapter 2.)

Tofu lives in the shadow of tempeh's nutritional profile. Minus the bacteria, it is of similar makeup but falls short in quantity due to its refinement.

Tempeh

The process of making tempeh from soybeans is both simple and complex: simple in the effort and equipment, complex in taking it through many stages on its way to being tempeh. First, whole dry soybeans are boiled, then soaked for 8 to 16 hours and drained. The hulls are loosened by rubbing them with the hands. Then water is added to cover so that the hulls will float to the surface and can easily be removed. The beans are boiled again for 20 to 30 minutes with vinegar or lactic acid, drained, and cooled before being mixed with a tempeh starter of *Rhizopus oligosporus* mold spores. After inoculation with this friendly bacterial culture, the beans are put in a container to incubate at a steady temperature for 22 to 26 hours. When tempeh is finished, there is a white fuzzy coating across the top. It feels like a baby's skin. The beans are bound by an almost invisible film. The aroma is fresh and nutty, the texture firm and dry.

Occasionally manufacturers include a grain in the process of making tempeh. My favorite combination is soy-rice tempeh. Other combinations, such as soy-quinoa, or soy-azuki bean, or soy-sea vegetable, have less appeal to me and a less dependable texture to work with. For more information on tempeh, including exact details on making your own, refer to *The Book of Tempeh* by William Shurtleff and Akiko Aoyagi.

Fresh tempeh stores well in the freezer and keeps up to a week to ten days refrigerated. Old tempeh carries a heavy smell and if you see pink or red streaks through the cake, put it in your garden's compost. However, black is a healthy streak to find.

Tofu

The process of making tofu, sometimes called bean curd or soy cheese, resembles that of making dairy cheese: a protein-rich milk merges with an agent that separates curds from whey, and then the whey is eliminated and the curds are pressed. Soy milk is prepared by grinding soaked hulled soybeans and cooking this mash with lots of water. After straining the bean's fiber from the liquid, elements of sea water and/or natural gypsum are used to curdle the soy milk. When pure, natural, food-grade elements are not available, manufacturers call upon sodium chloride and calcium sulfate to be curdling agents. After the whey is drained off, the curds are pressed into shape to form tofu.

The different kinds of tofu available in markets and tofu shops range from silken soft to medium firm to extra firm. Another form, deep-fried tofu or *age,* is a fully cooked selection. Age is a puffy, sometimes soft, sometimes crisp form of tofu. Purchased in Oriental markets, this product is a great candidate for stuffing, stews, or slices as a decorative addition to a vegetable dish.

Although dried tofu is available, I haven't found an appetizing reason to work with it. Sometimes manufacturers grill the cube of pressed tofu. This gives it an extra edge of usability and firmness, reducing the chalky aftertaste of uncooked tofu. Grilling feels like a pretreatment to me. Other pretreatments for tofu are boiling and steaming. These methods also reduce the chalky taste.

Often you can interchange the kinds of tofu in dishes. Silken tofu blends easily into a creamy sauce and performs well in combination with regular or firm tofu in casserole-style dishes where you want to mimic the texture of cottage or ricotta cheese. It is delicate and melts in your mouth. Medium tofu is most versatile, offering a texture that works as a slab for sandwiches and responds to deep-frying and marinating. It is not so firm that it avoids absorbing the flavors of the cooking methods. Firm tofu would be my first choice for the grill simply because it holds its shape most consistently. If you need to make julienne-style strips with tofu, firm is your best choice.

To store tofu, cover it with water in a closed container and refrigerate. If you have more quantity than you can use in a week, freeze the package of tofu as it is. Note, however, that freezing changes the texture of tofu dramatically and makes it become porous and spongy. It is a delightful texture for all cooking methods except purees. So if you are planning to use frozen tofu for a spread, sauce, or dip, *don't*! However, deep-frying, baking, refrying, braising and marinating all work really well with frozen tofu. Personally, I like this food prepared simply and individually. However, it makes a great ingredient in dishes that require cheese, such as lasagna, enchiladas, and filo pies. There are versions of these dishes in this book.

Cooking Methods for Tofu and Tempeh

PRETREATMENTS:
Parboil, steam, *freeze*
FIRST-STAGE METHODS:
Blending, boiling, marinating, refrying, deep-frying, baking

Pretreatments for tofu and tempeh are particularly crucial when serving dips and spreads. An uncooked bean dish is dangerous and these processed foods are just that, uncooked. To make spreads and dips (the blending method), it is important to parboil or steam. Freezing is optional for tofu. There are only two reasons to freeze tofu: as a method of preservation, or to change the texture to one that contradicts what people normally think of tofu.

PARBOILING

Parboiling allows the possibilities of having flavors infiltrate the bland bean cakes. Choose spices and colorful exotic cooking liquids to be artistic with this plain food. This liquid can be a seasoned marinade, spicy water, or a combination of water and other cooking liquids, such as wine or mirin. Cover tofu or tempeh with cooking liquid and boil gently for about 15 to 20 minutes. Tofu will be firmer and tempeh could be quite loose. Strain the excess liquid and let the cake drain or press the extra liquid out (see illustration) if you are in a hurry.

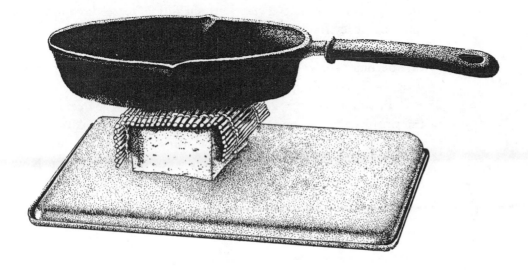

1. *Place slabs of tofu on an inverted bowl or tray.*
2. *Place a mat or plate on top of the tofu with a medium-heavy object on the center.*
3. *Excess water from the tofu will drain off. Allow at least 20 minutes.*

STEAMING

This method has the food sitting above hot water. Use a steaming rack in a pot or in a pressure cooker. I often pressure-steam for 10 minutes to hurry the process along; otherwise allow at least 20 minutes in a regular pot. The cake should be quite firm when finished and may not need pressing. Pressing is useful when the beans have absorbed extra liquid.

FREEZING

Freezing is primarily a pretreatment for tofu. It originated during the cold winters in the mountains of northern China. Combined with drying, it gives this product a very long shelf life. Freeze-dried tofu feels like emergency food to me and not so sensuous. But when you simply freeze fresh tofu at home, it has magnificent possibilities. The texture becomes chewy. It actually looks like a sponge and that's what it does—it sponges up flavor.

Place a sealed package of tofu, with water, into the freezer. It will transform within 12 hours, but will keep many months. To defrost it, put the whole sealed package into warm water and let it melt away the ice. Then open the package and press out the excess water. Now frozen tofu is ready for a first-stage method.

Teriyaki Tempeh Burgers

I normally don't try to make a vegetarian look-alike to meat dishes, but this combination of ingredients makes a succulent morsel to lay into a warm bun. This dish uses the braising method (starting with oil and adding liquid in the later stages of cooking).

Serves 4

1. Slice the tempeh into slabs about ½ inch thick.

2. Heat a heavy skillet to medium high. Add the light sesame oil and tempeh. Cook for 10 minutes. Add the dark sesame oil as you flip the tempeh to the other side and cook for 10 minutes. Reduce the fire as needed.

3. Mix the garlic, ginger juice, tamari, mirin, vinegar, and water together in a bowl or measuring cup. Pour over the tempeh and cover immediately. Reduce the heat if the pan will hold the temperature.

4. Turn the tempeh so that both sides absorb the braising liquid.

5. Serve hot in a grilled or steamed bun.

SERVING SUGGESTIONS: Serve with hot or cold potato salad and a corn soup.

8 ounces soybean tempeh (1 package)
3 tablespoons light sesame oil
3 tablespoons dark sesame oil
1 teaspoon minced garlic
1 teaspoon ginger juice (grate a 1-inch chunk of fresh ginger; squeeze the fiber to extract the juice)
2 tablespoons tamari
1 tablespoon mirin
1 tablespoon rice vinegar
1 tablespoon water
4 buns
Tomatoes, onions, and lettuce for filling the buns

The Process

BEANS: Medium or firm tofu could easily replace tempeh.
COOKING LIQUID: Sake could replace mirin. Any other vinegar could replace rice vinegar. The added water allows the braising liquid a chance to infuse the tempeh. Without this small amount of water, the combination of salt seasoning and fire would dry up the liquid before it cooks into the bean.
SALT SEASONING: It would be hard to call this a teriyaki-flavored dish without using tamari or shoyu as the salt seasoning.
OIL: You could use just light or dark sesame—no need to use both—or opt for canola or safflower oil.
HERBS AND SPICES: Garlic and ginger, a traditional combination, give this dish a powerful and familiar taste.
VEGETABLES: Use your favorite burger garnishes.

FIRST STAGE:
Braise
BEANS:
Tempeh
COOKING LIQUID:
Water, mirin, rice vinegar
SALT SEASONING:
Tamari
OIL:
Dark and light sesame oil
HERBS/SPICES:
Ginger, garlic
VEGETABLES:
Trimmings for burgers

Tempeh Stroganoff

1 pound large mushrooms
2 to 3 tablespoons olive
  oil
½ teaspoon sea salt
8 ounces soy tempeh,
  sliced ¼ inch
  thin x 3 x ½ inch wide
3 to 6 tablespoons ghee
3 tablespoons umeboshi
  vinegar
1 tablespoon ghee
3 cups thinly sliced onions
½ teaspoon vegetable salt
½ teaspoon black pepper
1 tablespoon dried basil
1 tablespoon paprika
2 tablespoons minced
  garlic
2 cups rice milk
¼ cup raw cashews
1 tablespoon fresh lemon
  juice

This lavish, sumptuous dish caters to mushroom lovers. Rich, succulent, juicy mushrooms contrast with crisp, tangy tempeh, all smothered in a luscious creamy sauce. By the time all the different stages have been prepared, this dish accumulates a generous quantity of fat. Please use your discretion. Also notice that this dish breaks some general rules about using more than one ingredient from each category.

Serves 4

1. Wash and dry the mushrooms and remove the stems. Place the caps in a baking dish. Pour olive oil across and around the mushrooms, then toss them with your hands to rub the oil evenly into their skins. Sprinkle the salt across the mushrooms and toss again, having the crystals of salt touch them evenly. Cover and bake at 350°F for 20 minutes or until the mushroom juice has come out into a puddle around them. Drain well, reserving the juice. Cut the mushrooms into large pieces, probably quarters.

2. Heat a large heavy-bottomed skillet over medium-high heat. Add 2 tablespoons ghee and place half the tempeh into the ghee. Cook until each side is darker in color and crisp. Repeat with remaining tempeh and ghee. Remove from the pan, slice the tempeh pieces in half vertically, and sprinkle them with umeboshi vinegar.

3. Add another tablespoon of ghee to the skillet and add the slivered onions. Move the onions around the ghee to seal them and then let them cook on a medium-high flame for 30 minutes or until they are brown. Stir once or twice to prevent burning but not so much that the onions don't brown.

4. Add the vegetable salt, pepper, basil, and paprika to the onions and cook together for 2 minutes. Add mushrooms. Combine the chopped garlic, rice milk, and cashews in a blender or food processor and blend for 3 minutes. Pour this over the onions and mushroom. Simmer together until the sauce thickens slightly, about 5 minutes. Add the tempeh carefully so that it doesn't break into pieces. Adjust the final substance with lemon and mushroom juice left over from baking the mushrooms. Cook for 5 minutes.

SERVING SUGGESTIONS: Serve hot over plain rice, couscous, or pasta. A clear, oil-free soup and salad would be good company.

The Process

BEANS: It is difficult to acquire the crispy texture of tempeh with another bean. It is possible, avoiding any effort to have this texture, that garbanzo beans would be good in place of tempeh. Tofu that has been frozen and deep-fried in the first stage would also be a possibility.

COOKING LIQUID: Rice milk can be replaced with water because the raw cashews blended with water make a nut milk. A touch of white wine might be a good addition to this dish, especially if it seems too salty.

SALT SEASONING: Three salt seasonings balance three oils. It may appear confusing at first glance, but think of each salt as having a different purpose. Sea salt brings the mushrooms to full flavor, vegetable salt integrates the onions and cooking liquid, and umeboshi vinegar helps cut through the rich ghee that tempeh needs to achieve its crisp texture. The effect is magnificent.

OIL: It is conceivable to use only ghee or only olive oil. But don't eliminate a nut milk base for the sauce. Almonds make a lower-fat milk than cashews, and pecans could offer a taste out of this world.

HERBS AND SPICES: Basil, pepper, and garlic bring both sweet and hot tastes to a dish that is rich in savory and sour flavors. Tarragon could substitute for basil. The other ingredients should stay.

VEGETABLES: The success of this dish depends on how perfectly the vegetables are cooked. Onions are standard and replaceable only by the whites of leeks. Mushrooms can not be substituted. You may want to add a decorative vegetable, such as red or yellow sweet peppers or parsley.

FIRST STAGE:
Refry
SECOND STAGE:
Slow cook, in sauce
BEANS:
Tempeh
COOKING LIQUID:
Rice milk, lemon juice
SALT SEASONING:
Umeboshi vinegar, sea salt, vegetable salt
OIL:
Olive oil, ghee, cashews
HERBS/SPICES:
Pepper, basil, paprika, garlic
VEGETABLES:
Mushrooms, onions

Millionaire's Tempeh Spread

8 ounces soy-rice tempeh
¾ cup celery (about 2 medium ribs), coarsely cut
1 cup green onions (about 4 medium), coarsely cut
3 tablespoons mayonnaise
1 tablespoon prepared mustard
4 tablespoons umeboshi vinegar
1 to 2 tablespoons dill weed
1½ cups pineapple cubes, drained
1 cup tamari roasted cashews

This golden dish was created for a family of great wealth who recognized value in simple food. The wide range of tastes moves from sweet to aromatic to nutty to tangy. Smooth, crunchy, soft, and hard textures keep the mouth interested. It is easy to make this textured dish into a paste, so don't let the processor run without your attention.

Yield: 4 cups

1. Steam the tempeh for 20 minutes (or 10 minutes under full pressure in a pressure cooker). Let cool.

2. In a food processor, combine celery, onions, tempeh, mayonnaise, mustard, umeboshi vinegar, dill weed and pineapple. Press the pulse tab about 24 times quickly to reach a coarse texture. Scrape down the sides to mix all ingredients evenly, and adjust the seasoning if necessary.

3. Add the cashews, and continue to process with the pulse tab to reach a consistency you like. Keep it chunky.

SERVING SUGGESTIONS: My favorite way to serve this spread is in a croissant with sprouts or Bibb lettuce. It can also be good on crackers or herb bread.

The Process

PRETREATMENT:
Pressure-steam
FIRST STAGE:
Blend (spread)
BEANS:
Tempeh
COOKING LIQUID:
None
SALT SEASONING:
Umeboshi vinegar
OIL:
Mayonnaise, cashews
HERBS/SPICES:
Mustard, dill
VEGETABLES:
Pineapple chunks, celery, green onions

BEANS: There is no alternative. This was specially designed for tempeh.
COOKING LIQUID: None.
SALT SEASONING: Umeboshi vinegar stands alone. There are no other options.
OIL: Mayonnaise provides the oil. If you choose not to use mayonnaise, try sesame oil or, better, tahini with lemon juice. Cashews also add oil.
HERBS AND SPICES: Dill, the representative herb, becomes a dominant flavor depending on how much is used. Dill works so well, I can't imagine a different herb in this dish.
VEGETABLES: Celery and onions provide a crunch but also contribute to a major part of the taste. As in potato salad, these two ingredients would be hard to replace. If you do, find something that is both crunchy and full-flavored, such as radishes and fennel.

TAMARI ROASTED CASHEWS: Place whole cashews on a pie plate in a preheated 350°F oven. Bake them until they are golden brown and the aroma fills your being. Turn them regularly even if they don't look like they are getting brown. Once the oil heats up inside then things happen quickly, so turn the nuts more often towards the end of the cooking time. Sprinkle the hot nuts with enough tamari to coat them moderately and toss in the pan as the liquid tamari dries on the hot nuts. Let cool before eating.

Tempeh Bacon

What draws one to bacon? The smoky flavor? Maybe. But most people are also attracted to the combination of fat and salt. This dish is for those days when you can handle that intense relationship. The quality of this protein is kinder to the body than that of a pig, and the sensuous quality of bacon is not lost.

6 tablespoons light
   sesame oil
½ teaspoon hickory
   flavoring
½ pound tempeh, sliced
   ⅛ inch thick
1 tablespoon tamari

Serves 4

1. Mix the oil and hickory flavoring in a bowl. Place the tempeh in the oil and turn to coat both sides.

2. Heat a large skillet over medium-high heat. Place the tempeh slices in the skillet and cook until crisp on both sides.

3. While tempeh is hot and preferably in the pan, sprinkle tamari evenly over the pieces, turning them carefully so that they do not break.

SERVING SUGGESTIONS: Serve with hot cereal in the morning, as a snack, or placed between lettuce and tomato on your favorite bread for a TLT sandwich.

The Process

BEANS: Try this with medium or firm tofu.
COOKING LIQUID: None, although you could marinate the tempeh first (see Teriyaki Tempeh Burgers, page 133).
SALT SEASONING: Tamari can be replaced with umeboshi vinegar.
OIL: Olive oil, ghee, or canola oil could substitute for the sesame oil.
HERBS AND SPICES: None. You could season the oil with cilantro, garlic, or ginger.
VEGETABLES: None.

FIRST STAGE:
Pan-fry
BEANS:
Tempeh
COOKING LIQUID:
None
SALT SEASONING:
Tamari
OIL:
Sesame oil
HERBS/SPICES:
Hickory flavoring
VEGETABLES:
None

Marinated Tofu

3 tablespoons dried onion flakes
1 tablespoon dried basil
1 tablespoon dried tarragon
1¼ teaspoons red pepper flakes
6 whole cloves
1 cup water
½ teaspoon salt
½ pound tofu, cubed
1½ tablespoons black sesame seeds (brown will work, if you are willing to forgo the accent color)
2 teaspoons fresh mint, minced
4 tablespoons fresh lemon juice
4 tablespoons fresh lime juice
1 teaspoon honey
Salt to taste

This unusual-looking tofu dish is speckled with red and black and chilled in a cool, sweet lemon-mint sauce. But don't be fooled by the chill; there is a distinct, warming aftertaste from hot pepper. Cut the tofu in small cubes for salads or in larger cubes to be spiked on toothpicks for an appetizer.

Yield: 1 cup

1. Combine the onion flakes, basil, tarragon, red pepper flakes, cloves, water, and ½ teaspoon salt in a saucepan. Boil for 2 minutes. Add the tofu cubes and simmer until most of the water is gone, about 15 minutes on medium heat. Pick out the tofu, leaving the liquid and herbs behind. Some herbs will cling to the tofu; this is good.

2. Toast the sesame seeds in a skillet, stirring or shaking constantly, until they will crush between your fingers. Transfer to a bowl or mortar and crush until most of the seeds are open.

3. In a bowl, mix the lemon juice, mint, honey, crushed sesame seeds and salt to fit. Add the tofu, mix, and chill or serve at room temperature.

SERVING SUGGESTIONS: Put cubes in salad or in a pasta dish. Serve among marinated vegetables as a side dish or specialty hors d'oeuvre.

The Process

BEANS: The flavors of this marinade would work with cooked white beans or garbanzo beans but the technique will be quite different. Cook the marinade as usual, but without the beans; then strain it over the beans and let the dish sit for several hours. Add the sesame seeds before serving.

COOKING LIQUID: I thought about using sherry or another wine to replace the water, but considering all the spices and herbs I thought I would see what those would do first. If you choose a different cooking liquid, such as mirin or beer, use it in combination with water because it would be too strong by itself. Lemon juice could be replaced with rice vinegar or lime juice.

SALT SEASONING: With sea salt, the colors and flavors stay clear. Tamari could work in the boiling part or miso in the marinade part, but the colors will change. You could design the dish around this if you include either paprika or turmeric in the boiling stage.

OIL: The only oil in this recipe as it stands comes from the sesame seeds, but they don't really count as fat. You could add dark sesame oil for additional flavor.

HERBS AND SPICES: Tofu is so bland, it makes a wonderful canvas for herbs and spices. On a whim, I chose this unusual combination knowing that I wanted it strong and multidirectional. I shot my wad on this one, so feel free to pick some alternatives.

VEGETABLES: The addition of cucumbers and radish would make a lovely salad for summer. Leave the skin on the cucumbers (assuming they are organic) so that the green contributes to this black, red, and white dish. Shredded carrot, beet, and/or leafy lettuce are other options. Combine this dish with baked carrots or squash in cooler months.

PRETREATMENT:
Boil
FIRST STAGE:
Marinate
BEANS:
Tofu
COOKING LIQUID:
Water, lemon juice
SALT SEASONING:
Sea salt
OIL:
Sesame seeds
HERBS/SPICES:
Mint, onion flakes, basil, tarragon, red pepper, cloves
VEGETABLES:
None
MISCELLANEOUS:
Honey

Marinated Baked Tofu
With Mango Chutney

½ pound tofu
1 teaspoon garlic minced
1 teaspoon ginger juice
2 tablespoons tamari
1 tablespoon mirin
1 tablespoon rice vinegar
¼ cup water
½ teaspoon sesame oil
¼ cup mango chutney

This outrageously easy dish can be prepared in two stages: fiirst the marinade, which can sit for up to 4 days, then baking.

Serves 2

1. Preheat the oven to 350°F. Cut the tofu into slabs ¼ to ½ inch thick, then into rectangles or triangles.

2. Combine the garlic, ginger, tamari, mirin, rice vinegar, and water in a saucepan. Add the tofu and boil until liquid is gone. If it's more convenient simply combine the tofu and marinade and refrigerate for 24 hours or more, then boil it when you have time.

3. Use the sesame oil to oil a baking pan. Lay the tofu in the baking pan, turning to coat it lightly with oil. Cover the top with chutney and bake for 20 minutes.

SERVING SUGGESTIONS: Serve with hot couscous, slow-cooked winter squash, and stir-fried onions and red peppers.

The Process

PRETREATMENT:
Boil
FIRST STAGE:
Bake
BEANS:
Tofu
COOKING LIQUID:
Water, mirin, rice vinegar
SALT SEASONING:
Tamari
OIL:
Sesame oil
HERBS/SPICES:
Garlic, ginger
VEGETABLES:
Chutney

BEANS: You could apply this dish to tempeh. Be careful to select a variety that will hold together; soy-rice or just soybean are the best choices.

COOKING LIQUID: Mirin can be replaced with any kind of wine or sake. Water keeps the alcohol and salt from evaporating too quickly and concentrating the salt too much.

SALT SEASONING: Tamari keeps the traditional flavors of this teriyaki-style marinade. Be inventive with an umeboshi or miso-mustard combination.

OIL: You can use as much or as little oil as you like in this dish. Brush it on the pan or pour it over the tofu. Just make sure there is some on both sides of the tofu.

HERBS AND SPICES: Garlic and ginger are spouses in this dish. Don't separate them unless you have to. Indian spices may be suitable to accompany the chutney.

VEGETABLES: Chutney fills this category. Some chutneys are made from fruits, others from vegetables. Tofu will like any of them, because tofu knows that alone it is next to nothing in taste.

Tofu Horseradish Dip

Delightfully creamy, white, and peppy, this dip can be made into an entirely different dish by changing the focus in the herbs/spices and vegetables categories. For example, emphasize such vegetables as roasted sweet red pepper or cucumbers. Or vary the herbs and spices with garlic or mint. This dip ages well. Give it several hours or a day to infuse.

Yield: 1 cup

Chop the shallot and celery finely in a food processor. Add the tofu, oil, horseradish, dill, and umeboshi vinegar and blend well. Chill for a minimum of 1 hour.

SERVING SUGGESTIONS: Use as a dip for carrots, peppers, zucchini, etc., or spread on crackers, French bread croutons, or pita bread.

1 medium shallot
½ cup sliced celery (1 large stalk)
½ pound tofu, boiled and pressed
2 tablespoons olive oil
1 to 2 heaping tablespoons prepared horseradish
1 teaspoon dill weed
2 tablespoons umeboshi vinegar

The Process

BEANS: Tofu and beans are interchangeable in this style of dip. Garbanzos, white beans, and almost any creamy bean will do.
COOKING LIQUID: You really don't want too much liquid, just enough of an accent liquid, such as lemon juice or vinegar, to balance the flavors.
SALT SEASONING: Umeboshi vinegar provides both the accent and the salt in this dish. It's a great choice for dramatizing bland tofu. Tamari turns the pure white color of tofu to a mucky tan, but white miso might work on occasion as a substitute.
OIL: Substitute sesame oil for olive oil.
HERBS AND SPICES: Horseradish rules. Dill balances its power just enough to keep your mouth interested for quite a while. For alternative herbs and spices, look to hot red peppers with mint or to garlic with fresh basil.
VEGETABLES: Shallots represent the onion family in this dip; green onions or garlic could easily substitute. Celery, the only other vegetable in this dish, could be accompanied by olives, cucumbers, or roasted red peppers.

PRETREATMENT:
Boil
FIRST STAGE:
Blend (dip)
BEANS:
Tofu
COOKING LIQUID:
None
SALT SEASONING:
Umeboshi vinegar
OIL:
Olive oil
HERBS/SPICES:
Horseradish, dill
VEGETABLES:
Shallots, celery

Frozen Tofu Krispies in Sweet and Sour Sauce

1 pound tofu, frozen,
  defrosted
¾ cup pineapple juice
2 tablespoons arrowroot
  powder
1½ tablespoons apple
  cider vinegar
1½ teaspoons pickling
  spices, crushed or
  ground
sea salt to fit
1 pinch beet powder
  (optional)
canola or safflower oil for
  deep-frying
Tamari or shoyu to fit
1 small sweet red pepper
2 cups pea pods,
  de-veined, steamed
1 small onion, boat
  shaped, steamed
1 cup pineapple, cubed
½ cup tamari roasted
  almonds

This dish offers great opportunity for variety in color and texture. Served with a grain, it becomes a meal in itself. The sauce is thick, verging on being a glaze. If you want it thinner, simply add more juice or cooking liquid and adjust the salt seasoning accordingly.

Serves 2–4

1. Press the tofu and drain off the excess water.

2. In a heavy-bottomed saucepan or skillet, combine pineapple juice, vinegar, arrowroot, pickling spices and salt. Stir well to dilute the arrowroot. Over medium-high heat, stir frequently until the sauce is clear, smooth, and thick. Remove from heat.

3. Heat deep-frying oil to 375°F or until you can see the surface move. (Please read about deep-frying on page 51.)

4. While oil is heating, cut the tofu twice through the middle into three pieces, keeping the layers in place, then cut across 3 times through the layers making strips.

5. Lower the strips into the oil a few at a time. Turn and remove as they brown and become crisp. Put them on a towel or paper bag to drain.

6. Sprinkle them with tamari or shoyu and put them in the sauce. Either let them sit until reheating for serving time or cook them for 10 minutes.

7. Before serving, reheat the sauce and tofu and toss in the steamed vegetables.

8. Garnish with slivered roasted almonds.

SERVING SUGGESTIONS: Serve hot or at room temperature over hot rice or buckwheat noodles.

The Process

BEANS: I usually use firm tofu for this dish. But I strongly suspect that other forms would work, creating a slightly different texture. Tempeh cut into small cubes would also be a great alternative.

COOKING LIQUID: The taste of this clear sauce depends on the flavor of the cooking liquid. Apple juice and raisin water (raisins soaked or boiled in warm water) are frequent substitutes for pineapple juice. If you have to, use water with a major sweetener, such as honey or rice syrup, to create the sweet liquid. Apple cider vinegar is my favorite accent liquid for bringing the sour flavor into this sauce but I am comfortable with rice vinegar and tempted to use a good raspberry vinegar. If you use umeboshi as the sour taste, it works better to use lemon or lime juice rather than a vinegar to increase the strength of flavor.

SALT SEASONING: I have chosen plain sea salt to integrate the flavors of the sauce, and tamari or shoyu to balance the oil in the tofu. Miso could be a substitute in combination with some sea salt, but be careful with umeboshi as a salt seasoning unless you work it in to represent the sour taste replacing vinegar.

OIL: Sometimes I combine the oils, using canola for its lightness and safflower for the flavor. At this point I don't have a strong preference, although safflower has more character. The nut garnish may or may not seem appropriate to you. Consider using roasted sunflower seeds or roasted cashews salted with umeboshi vinegar when they are hot.

HERBS AND SPICES: This dish uses pickling spices, which are a combination of bay leaf, cloves, allspice, mustard, dill, cinnamon, and caraway. A sweet grouping accents the sweet flavor of this sauce. I also like to use a strong dose of fresh ginger juice in place of this wild combination of flavors. Simply grate the ginger (preferably on a fine-toothed ginger grater) and squeeze the juice into the sauce. One inch of fresh ginger, grated and squeezed, should be the minimum. Garlic is always an option.

VEGETABLES: It is important to precook the vegetables so that they are perfect in themselves before they mingle in the sauce. Options for vegetables include napa cabbage, green onions, thin carrots, broccoli, cauliflower, asparagus, celery, mushrooms, squash, leafy greens, green beans, lotus root and probably more. Pineapple acts as a vegetable in this dish. If a fruit and vegetable combination is difficult for you, simply leave it out. You may want to modify some of the direct sweetness by putting more rice syrup in the sauce.

PRETREATMENT:
Freeze
FIRST STAGE:
Deep-fry
BEANS:
Tofu
COOKING LIQUID:
Pineapple juice
SALT SEASONING:
Sea salt, tamari/shoyu
OIL:
Canola or safflower
HERBS/SPICES:
Pickling spices
VEGETABLES:
Sweet red peppers, onions, pea pods

Tofu, Zucchini, and Pecan Lasagna

8 cups tomato sauce (see recipe page 146)
12–14 strips dried lasagna
2½ cups soft tofu
2 cloves garlic (optional)
1 cup pecans
¾ cup fresh basil, chopped
5 tablespoons white miso
2 cups zucchini, shredded
3 tablespoons olive oil
Vegetable salt to fit
½ cup chopped pecans, for topping

Pecans make this mono-textured dish exciting. But they also turn the tofu a light purple. Especially the way this lasagna is layered, tomato sauce does not reach the tofu mixture directly. You may want to assemble this dish by repeating the pattern of layers instead of sandwiching all the filling between noodles, as described here. If you are a cheese eater, replace the nuts with cheese, or use them both.

Serves 8–10

1. Preheat the oven to 350°F. Lay 4 cups of sauce in the bottom of a 9 × 12-inch baking dish. Place 1 layer of uncooked noodles on top of the sauce, overlapping them slightly.

2. Mix the tofu, garlic, 1 cup pecans, basil, and miso together in a food processor until smooth. Spread half of the tofu mixture over the noodles. Lay the zucchini on top of the tofu and sprinkle with the olive oil and vegetable salt. Spread the remaining tofu mixture on top of the zucchini.

3. Arrange the remaining lasagna noodles across the top of the casserole. Cover these with 4 cups of sauce and sprinkle coarsely cut pecans on top. Cover with oven-proof plastic or parchment and then seal tightly with foil; bake until the pasta is tender, 30 to 40 minutes.

SERVING SUGGESTIONS: Serve with a vegetable salad, with or without soup, and perhaps a loaf of French bread to complete or embellish the meal.

The Process

BEANS: Theoretically, other bean spreads could be used in a similar way: tempeh, garbanzo pâté, spreads, or refried beans could conceivably be placed between layers of pasta and baked in a sauce. Alternatives to layers of pasta would be tortillas, both corn and flour, and leafy greens, such as collards or cabbage leaves.

COOKING LIQUID: In this dish, tomato sauce is the cooking liquid. If you purchase tomato sauce or if yours is too thick, add some Marsala wine or water to dilute it.

SALT SEASONING: Although there is salt in the sauce, the tofu and vegetable filling need additional salt. I chose vegetable salt for its complexity of taste as well its ability to help the innermost layer of raw vegetables to become cooked. If you use plain sea salt here, sprinkle a layer of extra herbs along with it. Stretching the imagination a bit, you'll find that miso adds some of the fermented quality of cheese.

OIL: Olive oil has no substitute in the traditional flavors of this dish. If using tortillas consider corn oil; for greens look to sesame. It is best to keep the oil relative to the flavor scheme of the ethnic tradition.

HERBS AND SPICES: Garlic is optional in this dish since the tomato sauce has many flavors. Basil fills the dull tofu. Other herbs could work as you change the sauce, vegetables, and beans.

VEGETABLES: Spinach is a common choice for vegetarian lasagna. Or pick another vegetable that becomes soft and moist, such as eggplant, mushrooms, peppers, or other summer squash or winter squash. Or you could precook more long-term vegetables like carrots or rutabagas. An abundant and very brown layer of slivered onions, cooked long to be sweet and translucent, would be heavenly in the center of this dish.

PRETREATMENT:
Boil, press
FIRST STAGE:
Bake (casserole)
PASTRY:
Lasagna noodles
BEANS:
Tofu
COOKING LIQUID:
Tomato sauce
SALT SEASONING:
Vegetable salt
OIL:
Olives, pecans
HERBS/SPICES:
Garlic, fresh basil
VEGETABLES:
Zucchini

Tomato Sauce

1/4–1/2 cup olive oil
3/4 cup whole garlic cloves
chopped
2 cups onions, diced
2 tablespoons (heaping)
dry oregano
2 tablespoons (heaping)
dry basil
1 tablespoon fennel,
crushed
2 (28-ounce) cans crushed
tomatoes
2 (28-ounce) cans whole
peeled tomatoes
1 tablespoon sea salt
2 medium bay leaves
1/2 cup Marsala wine
1 tablespoon olive oil
2 cups mushrooms,
slivered
1/2 teaspoon black pepper

This is one of my versions of tomato sauce. Variations lean toward the addition of sweet spices, such as cinnamon and cloves, and sometimes shredded cabbage.

Yield: 10 cups

1. Over medium-high flame, heat a heavy-bottomed 6–8 quart pot. Add oil and garlic; cook for a few minutes.

2. Add onions, oregano, basil, and fennel and cook together for about 3 minutes.

3. Add tomatoes, sea salt, and bay leaves.

4. Heat a skillet on high. Add 1 tablespoon olive oil and mushrooms. Cook on high until mushrooms are squeeking, dry, golden brown, and not slippery.

5. Add mushrooms. Adjust salt seasoning, add Marsala wine and pepper to taste, and cook for about 6 hours over medium-low heat, covered, with a flame tamer.

Frozen Tofu Baked in Barbecue Sauce

1 pound frozen tofu,
defrosted and drained
Light sesame oil to coat
1 1/2 cups Barbecue Sauce
(recipe follows)

This is a simple, uncomplicated, time-efficient dish with familiar flavors and textures. Frozen tofu makes a wonderful, surprising texture.

Serves 4

1. Slice the tofu 1/4 inch thick, then cut into the desired shape – squares, slabs, or triangles.

2. Put a little sesame oil into your hands and rub it over the tofu, or if you don't want to touch the food, brush it on with a pastry brush especially when cooking in quantity. Lay tofu in oiled baking pan and smother with barbecue sauce. Cover and bake for 30–40 minutes or until the sauce has cooked through the tofu. Uncover and cook another 10 minutes to brown.

SERVING SUGGESTIONS: Serve with a hot grain dish and cooked vegetables.

The Process

BEANS: Tempeh could replace the frozen and thawed tofu, although then I would boil the tempeh in a teriyaki marinade as a pretreatment.
COOKING LIQUID: Barbecue sauce provides enough liquid; you don't really want too much of a watery ingredient in this style of dish.
SALT SEASONING: The sauce provides plenty of salt. Add tamari for a deeper color if you want more salt.
OIL: Olive oil or canola oil would also work. The idea here is to seal the edges of the tofu so that it bakes to a golden tan.
HERBS AND SPICES: Hickory flavoring in the barbecue sauce carries this dish. Garlic and basil in a sun-dried tomato sauce would be a good alternative.
VEGETABLES: Tomatoes are dominant in the sauce. Change the sauce to a roasted red pepper and olive puree for variations.

PRETREATMENT:
Freeze
FIRST STAGE:
Bake
BEANS:
Tofu
COOKING LIQUID:
Barbecue sauce
SALT SEASONING:
In barbecue sauce
OIL:
Light sesame oil
HERBS/SPICES:
In barbecue sauce
VEGETABLES:
Onions

Barbecue Sauce

Yield: 2 cups

Combine the ingredients in a heavy-bottomed saucepan and cook over medium-low heat for 15 minutes, stirring frequently.

1 can (6 ounces) tomato paste
6 ounces water (fill can)
3 tablespoons brown rice miso
3 tablespoons prepared mustard
1 tablespoon prepared horseradish
½ teaspoon hickory flavoring (liquid smoke)
3 tablespoons sucanat (natural brown sugar)
1 teaspoon sea salt
1½ tablespoons apple cider vinegar
2 tablespoons barley malt

Savory Tofu Pie

1 tablespoon ghee
 (clarified butter)
½ cup diced onion
1 cup slivered green onions
1 cup cubed carrots
2 cups diced red potatoes
¾ cup thinly sliced celery
2 teaspoons vegetable salt
1 teaspoon poultry
 seasoning
1 teaspoon thyme
2 cups medium or firm
 tofu, diced
1 cup fresh or frozen corn
 kernels
1 cup fresh or frozen green
 peas
3 tablespoons unbleached
 white flour
1 tablespoon arrowroot
 flour
2 cups cool water
½ teaspoon apple cider
 vinegar
1 tablespoon tamari
½ teaspoon black pepper
2 sheets (8 × 10-inch)
 pre-rolled puff pastry
 (Pepperidge Farm),
 room temperature
Fresh rosemary to garnish

Pot pie, an American family favorite, brings staple vegetables together in a light sauce while they bake in a rich, light, and flaky crust. These simple, everyday ingredients gather intensity from the long slow-cooking process before the pie is baked. This recipe has an abundance of vegetables; you may want to reduce the total volume if they seem overwhelming.

Serves 4–6

1. Melt the ghee in a large skillet over medium-high heat. Add the onion and green onions and cook for 2 minutes or until translucent. Add the carrots and cook for 3 minutes, turning occasionally to brown all sides. Add the potatoes, mixing them with the other vegetables completely, and cook 3 to 5 minutes, turning them to avoid burning.

2. Reduce the heat to medium. Add the celery, vegetable salt, poultry seasoning, and thyme and cook for 15 minutes, turning just often enough to allow the vegetables to brown but not burn. Add the tofu, corn, and peas.

3. Mix the flour, arrowroot, water, vinegar, tamari, and black pepper in a bowl or cup. Pour the mixture over the cooked vegetables and stir to the bottom of the skillet, releasing the flavors that are stuck there into the sauce. Heat and stir until the sauce is clear. Remove from the heat.

4. Preheat the oven to 350°F. Roll the puff pastry sheets, one at a time, to 10 by 14 inches. Lay one pastry sheet in an 8–10-inch baking pan, letting the excess hang over the edges. Poke holes in the bottom crust with a fork. Bake for 10 minutes.

5. Remove the pan from the oven and spread the vegetable mixture evenly in the shell. Lay the other sheet of pastry on top, tucking in the corners and edges. Poke holes through the top crust and bake for 30 minutes.

6. Remove the pie from the oven and cut into serving sizes. Lay fresh rosemary over the cuts and return the pie to the oven to bake for 15 more minutes.

SERVING SUGGESTIONS: This is a complete meal by itself, but a leafy green salad would help balance the energetics of ingredients and cooking methods.

The Process

BEANS: Garbanzo beans or any light-colored bean would be a good substitute for tofu. Precooked tempeh would also be a possibility.

COOKING LIQUID: The water released by the vegetables forms a kind of vegetable stock in the skillet, which becomes the sauce. Apple cider vinegar could be replaced with another light-colored vinegar such as rice or raspberry, or lemon juice, which gives a lighter dimension to the root vegetables and earthy herbs.

SALT SEASONING: Vegetable salt provides an additional round of flavors while helping to draw out the best taste of the vegetables in this dish. Tamari helps the color as well and gives a wine-like taste. If you use wine in the cooking liquid in combination with water, then you will probably not need tamari.

OIL: Ghee has the ability to cook slowly, unlike oils that tend to increase the speed at which a vegetable cooks. But if you don't have any, use light sesame or olive oil.

HERBS AND SPICES: The dance of sage, rosemary, and thyme is an old one. Whatever blend of herbs you choose, be sure it includes thyme. Thyme can easily stand on its own in this dish.

VEGETABLES: Vegetables in this dish can vary according to season. Try combinations such as zucchini and tomatoes in summer, rutabaga and burdock in winter, or asparagus and artichokes in spring.

FIRST STAGE:
Bake (casserole)
BEANS:
Tofu
PASTRY:
Puff pastry
COOKING LIQUID:
Apple cider vinegar
SALT SEASONING:
Vegetable salt, tamari
OIL:
Ghee
HERBS/SPICES:
Poultry seasoning, thyme, pepper, rosemary
VEGETABLES:
Onions, green onions, carrots, potatoes, celery, corn, peas

Red Lacy Tofu

1 (8-ounce) package firm
  tofu
2 cups water
1 small red onion
¼ cup tamari
½ cup pastry flour
2 teaspoons beet root
  powder
½ cup cold water
3 tablespoons light
  sesame oil

The glorious ingredient of this dish is beet root powder. I stumbled upon it when I wanted to decorate Martha's birthday cake. Look for it in the bulk herb section of natural food markets. Somehow it ended up in some tempura batter instead. And what a surprise! Bright red, tasteful, and delicate, this ingredient is appropriate for tofu. It caught my children's attention immediately. But you don't have to use it. You can make the batter with pastry flour and maybe some wheat germ. Or, equally delicious, you don't have to use the batter at all.

Serves: 3

1. Press the tofu gently, keeping the large rectangle shape. Slice into ¼-inch-thick slabs. Bring the water, onion, and tamari to a gentle boil. Add the sliced tofu, cover, and cook gently for 15 to 20 minutes. Drain well and cool.

2. Mix the flour and beet root powder in a flat bowl. Add the water and mix well to form a batter.

3. Heat a large skillet over medium-high heat. Add oil. Dip the tofu slices in the batter and lay them in the hot oil. Let the first side cook until it is crisp, turn, and cook until crisp on the other side. Serve hot.

SERVING SUGGESTIONS: This beautiful dish is delicious, featured all by itself as a side to any grain and vegetable dish. Or it could be placed on an open-face sandwich with sprouts, lettuce, and marinated carrots.

The Process

BEANS: Firm or grilled tofu works best for maintaining the slab shape through a bit of handling. If you are not sure if your tofu is firm enough, try to pick up a slice by the corner to check its strength. If it seems too soft, use this tofu for a different dish.

COOKING LIQUID: Water and onion create a vegetable stock with a light fragrant scent to permeate the bland tofu. Other ingredients could alter this delicate taste making it stronger or equally delicate. For instance, white or yellow onion, leek, or shallot could replace red onion for a similar flavor. Ginger or jalapeños could bring some heat into the dish, and fennel, cinnamon, or cloves would bring sweetness. If you design a cooking liquid here, either keep your focus on one taste so that the beauty of simple tofu is not confused, or build a complex group of tastes, such as the Marinated Tofu recipe on page 138.

OIL: Light sesame oil is a compatible flavor with tofu. It has enough flavor to add to the bland character of this soy product. Dark sesame oil or ghee would also be delicious. Olive oil feels too fruity to me for this dish, but it would work.

SALT SEASONING: Tamari is frequently put on fried tofu at the end of cooking. Here it goes gracefully into the cooking liquid so that it is part of the piece of tofu and not just added on top.

HERBS AND SPICES: There really aren't any in this dish as I show it here. But frequently I add dry herbs to the flour. Oregano, garlic powder, basil, and tarragon are my favorites. Curry powder would be interesting, if you like curry.

PRETREATMENT:
Boil
FIRST STAGE:
Pan-fry
BEANS:
Tofu
COOKING LIQUID:
Onion water
SALT SEASONING:
Tamari
OIL:
Sesame oil
HERBS/SPICES:
Beet root powder
VEGETABLES:
Onions

Herbal Tofu Toast

2 tablespoons light
   sesame oil
2 cups slivered onions
1 cup julienne carrots
6 cups shredded savoy
   cabbage (1 small head)
1 tablespoon dried basil
1 teaspoon sea salt
1 pound tofu, drained and
   pressed
5 tablespoons tamari

Tofu, surrounded by a leafy green vegetable, onions, and savory herbs, absorbs many sweet, aromatic flavors. This dish can be elegant as a light summer dinner or a Sunday brunch. If you eat eggs, you may want to scramble eggs in the tofu and vegetables. This is the only dish I can think of where it works to cook cabbage with beans, and only because the beans have been transformed into tofu.

Serves 6

1. Heat a heavy skillet over medium-high heat. Add the oil and onions and cook for 5 minutes or until onions are brown, limp, and clear. Add the carrots and cook for another 3 minutes. Then add cabbage, stirring it into the other vegetables. Sprinkle basil and salt evenly around the skillet, mixing well. Cover, reduce the heat to medium-low, and cook for another 5 minutes.

2. Crumble the pressed tofu into the vegetables and pour tamari over the tofu. Mix into the vegetables, cover and cook for 10 minutes.

SERVING SUGGESTIONS: Serve warm or at room temperature over 6 toasted English muffins, other toast, or rice crackers. Use mayonnaise or make a nut sauce for an optional topping.

The Process

BEANS: Tofu is crumbly and fits nicely amongst the cooked vegetables. Whole garbanzo beans could be an interesting option.

COOKING LIQUID: None required; the cabbage gives off plenty of moisture.

SALT SEASONING: Umeboshi vinegar or light miso make reasonable alternatives to tamari. But sea salt should be used to help sweeten the vegetables.

OIL: Ghee or olive oil can replace sesame.

HERBS AND SPICES: I like to focus on one particular herb, such as basil, tarragon, thyme, or rosemary. But there is no reason not use several, or include some of the Indian spices, such as garam masala or asafetida. Put herbs and spices in the oil before the vegetables.

VEGETABLES: This flexible category dictates the entire impact of the dish. Swiss chard, kale, collard greens, green cabbage, purple cabbage, and zucchini are all possible alternatives to savoy cabbage. Shallots can be included but try to use onion anyway. Green onions could take the place of white or yellow onions.

FIRST STAGE:
Refry
BEAN:
Tofu
COOKING LIQUID:
None
SALT SEASONING:
Sea salt, tamari
OIL:
Light sesame oil
HERBS/SPICES:
Basil
VEGETABLES:
Onions, carrots

Clear Soup With Tofu

4 cups water

3 inches kombu sea
vegetable

3 inches fresh ginger,
sliced

1 tablespoon fresh mint,
minced (optional)

8 ounces tofu, pressed and
cut into small cubes

¼ teaspoon sea salt

¼ cup tamari, or to taste

¼ cup green onions, white
and green parts sliced
very thin

The word *clear* in the title of this style of soup has a triple meaning to me: uncluttered, energetically etheric, and usually having no oil. Making clear soups is a high art, balancing just a few ingredients, each having an essential role in the structure of a simple clear broth. This is a wonderful canvas for tofu and strips of decorative vegetables. Changing the cooking liquids and salt seasoning makes the soup distinct. Miso soup, tamari broth, hot and sour soup – all come from this style and technique.

Serves 6

1. Bring the water, kombu, and ginger to a rapid boil. Reduce the heat to a slow boil, add the mint, and cook for 7 to 10 minutes.

2. Strain, removing the kombu, ginger, and as much of the mint that departs naturally.

3. Add the tofu cubes and sea salt and cook 2 more minutes.

4. Add the tamari and green onions to the hot broth just before serving.

SERVING SUGGESTIONS: This is delicious as a first course for any grain and vegetable meal. It may also be served at room temperature or chilled.

The Process

FIRST STAGE:
Boil

SECOND STAGE:
None

BEANS:
Tofu

COOKING LIQUID:
Water

SALT SEASONING:
Tamari, sea salt

OIL:
None

HERBS/SPICES:
Ginger, mint

VEGETABLES:
Green onions

BEANS: Tofu is the only choice.

COOKING LIQUID: Water is simple, clear, and ready to show off all the flavors that enter the pot. You could also include small portions of mirin, sake, rice vinegar, lime juice, or vegetable stock.

SALT SEASONING: Change the salt seasoning from tamari to miso and you have miso soup. Did you notice in the recipe that tamari is added after everything else has cooked? Do that with miso also. Boiling miso does not affect the taste, but the little clouds of friendly bacteria that form when miso is heated are reported beneficial for balancing radiation, and boiling destroys this property.

Boiling the salt seasoning often reduces the liquid volume, making the dish saltier than you had intended. Umeboshi vinegar is a delightful alternative, stimulating the sour parts of our being with a strong astringent kick.

OIL: None.

HERBS AND SPICES: Fresh ginger and fresh mint are both strong flavors and would stand well on their own. Another flavor that enhances the clear cooking liquid is lemon zest. Avoid the white part of the lemon peel and just use the external pores. Play with all kinds of flavors—cilantro, rosemary, garlic—but keep the soup simple and clear.

VEGETABLES: Kombu sea vegetable reacts with the simple ingredients to bring about their very best flavors. Since it is a crucial ingredient to the strength of the cooking liquid, I recommend you always use it unless you create a special soup stock from other vegetables, such as mushrooms, onions, leeks, and cauliflower.

Tofu, Feta, and Greens Baked in Filo

Spanakopita and spinach pie are role models for this dish. This recipe is the only one in this book that includes eggs and cheese. Feel free to eliminate both; the dish still works. But these two ingredients lend such a special sensuality to tofu and the dish in general, I couldn't resist bringing them to you. Complete with grain, vegetables, and protein, this is a one-dish meal.

Serves 6

1 cup onion, diced
3 to 4 cups tender kale, chopped fine
3 cups broccoli, minced
1 tablespoon dry basil
2 cups firm tofu, pressed and drained
2 cups feta cheese
2 eggs, beaten
½ teaspoon pepper
3 tablespoons umeboshi vinegar
14 filo pastry leaves (about ⅔ pound)
½ cup ghee (approximately)

1. Preheat the oven to 350°F. Melt 2 tablespoons of the ghee in a skillet over medium heat. Add the onion and cook until soft. Add the kale, cook for a minute, and add the broccoli; cook just until the brightness of the vegetables comes out, but don't overcook. Remove from the heat.

2. In a 3-quart bowl, crumble the tofu and feta. Add the eggs, dried basil, pepper, and umeboshi vinegar. Add the cooked vegetables.

3. Melt the remaining ghee in a small saucepan. Line a 9 × 13-inch baking pan with a sheet of filo and brush with a sparse layer of ghee. Repeat, making 6 layers in all.

4. Smooth half the vegetable-tofu mixture on top of the sixth sheet of filo. Top with 4 more filo sheets, brushing each layer lightly with ghee.

5. Spread the remaining tofu mixture over the filo. Place the remaining 4 sheets of filo pastry on top, brushing each with ghee. Fold in the corners, using ghee to sort of paste them down. You may have to tuck them in. Brush the top with a finishing touch of ghee, then make a few delicate slashes through the top crust with a sharp knife. Bake until golden brown, 30 to 40 minutes.

SERVING SUGGESTIONS: A relish dish provides crunch, color, and a raw component to the meal.

The Process

FIRST STAGE:
Bake (casserole)
BEANS:
Tofu
PASTRY:
Filo
COOKING LIQUID:
None
SALT SEASONING:
Umeboshi vinegar
OIL:
Ghee
HERBS/SPICES:
Basil, pepper
VEGETABLES:
Onions, kale, broccoli

BEANS: The light texture and qualities of tofu are hard to replace, so for variations rely on herbs, spices, and vegetables.

COOKING LIQUID: None required. If you do not use the umeboshi salt seasoning, you will need an accent liquid, such as rice vinegar or lemon or lime juice, plus salt. Use the taste and smell test in building your dish.

SALT SEASONING: Umeboshi vinegar is the first choice in this dish. But tamari and miso could also be delicious. You will need an accent liquid if you choose an alternative salt seasoning.

HERBS AND SPICES: Basil stands alone as a delicate flavor. Filo has an extremely delicate personality, so I choose light, sweet flavors, and not too many. Fennel, tarragon, or dill could replace basil. Garlic rarely hurts a bean dish and practically rescues tofu. If you only use tofu without feta cheese, increase the numbers of herbs and spices.

VEGETABLES: Kale and broccoli provide a major contribution to this main course dish. Fresh corn and red peppers or zucchini and spinach make good alternative combinations.

Appendix

Cookware

Cookware for bean cookery begins with a pot for first-stage methods. This can be a pressure cooker, an electric crock cooker, or a saucepan with a very good seal at the lid. Flame tamers prevent scorching the bottom, so, unless you like a constant smoky flavor to your beans, use one when pressure cooking. Second-stage methods require skillets, open baking pans, baking dishes with lids, saucepans, soup pots, and bowls, plus miscellaneous tools for blending and mixing, and a pâté pan for perfect bean pâtés.

In choosing pots and pans consider the metal elements and their performance abilities. Heat either moves through metal or is generated by vibration of the crystal structures in ceramic or glass material. In a direct heat source (stove top), metal cookware is more responsive to change in temperature than ceramic, whose qualities respond best to oven methods where the heat is slow and steady. In fact, some ceramic and glass cookware may break with quick changes in temperature.

Some metals are too reactive and leak into the food. Witness this in cast iron pots with rusty patches or tarnished copper and silver. A thin-surfaced pot increases the mobility of these elements, sometimes affecting the color of the food. Look for stable metal in your cookware, which means alloy combinations that create the best possible conductivity and immobility.

Cast iron pots receive heat quickly and thoroughly and hold the temperature in a steady, even state. As the surface of this metal meets water and air, iron reaches for the surface and deposits itself in the form of rust. Where most other metal surfaces protect themselves from rusting with an oxidized coating, cast iron has no protection. Seasoning a cast iron pan creates this protective coating. The process is simple: heat the pan evenly in the oven and line it with a generous amount of oil. Over several hours, the oil saturates the pores in the metal, sealing it from exposure to the oxygen in air or water.

Stainless steel is iron combined with chromium and carbon. It's pretty and shiny, and also stable (it does not react chemically with the food). For natural-food cookery, stainless pans made from heavy-gauge metal are best.

Clay (earthenware, stoneware, terra cotta) is a most appealing material for bean cookery. Clay pots are especially good for baking and as the inserts in electric crock cookers, where their elemental components can be warmed and cooled evenly and gently.

PRESSURE COOKERS

I have heard some amusing pressure cooker stories that broadcast fear in awesome proportions. But after using a pressure cooker about every other day for twenty years, I trust them. Modern pressure cookers have many safety features to prevent any explosions. Of course, I have pushed the limits on capacity, but if you pay attention to a few details, little can go wrong. First of all, the inner seal should be in good shape, without nicks or food embedded in the rubber. The hole where steam escapes should be clean. And don't fill the pot more than two-thirds full. Some pressure cookers need to be brought up to pressure more slowly than others. In general pressure cookers leak too much if the flame is too hot to begin with. But most quality pressure cookers are responsive to fast heat and easy to take down without impending doom. New models have at least two safety release mechanisms.

Purchase a stainless steel or enamel pressure cooker that has a heavy, smooth bottom so that you can sauté in it before you cook and so that the beans cook gently and evenly. I also like a weighty lid and the ability to maintain pressure without any sound. Some pressure cookers claim they can cook split peas. And, indeed, they can. But most pressure cookers do not manage this partial (split) bean very well. If your supplier doesn't say it will cook split peas, don't try it.

ELECTRIC CROCK COOKER

The most delightful thing about Crockpots (actually a brand name, but used by many as a generic term) is the ceramic inner bowl that holds the beans. This earthy material is chemically stable and well matched for nature's food. Most pots have at least two speeds, high and low, a glass cover, and an aluminum casing to hold the clay pot. The aluminum holder never touches the food or affects its quality. The glass top is usually steamy so that looking inside still requires removing the lid. And although the speed records high, it never gets too hot or conducts the heat too quickly.

SKILLET

A cast iron or stainless steel skillet is essential for the refry method. I prefer a weighty bottom because it results in less scorching and even temperature, treating the food more kindly than a thin bottom pan. Don't be fooled by stick resistant coatings. Go for the real, elemental, metal. Make sure your skillet's lid provides a good seal; anything stuck to the bottom of the pan will steam loose in a few minutes when the skillet is covered.

BAKING PANS

There are three kinds of baking pans required for bean cookery: a covered baking dish for casseroles, an open-topped baking pan for pasta and pastry-lined dishes, and a soufflé dish or special baking pan for bean pâtés. My preference when baking beans in a sauce is pottery, stoneware or terra cotta. Enamel lined steel works beautifully also.

Casserole and filled pastry dishes work best in open shallow pans. They vary from rectangular glass to ceramic-lined steel. Stoneware or terra cotta are also good choices.

Pâtés require a special shaped pot; not that it has to be a rectangle or circle, but it has to have a companion piece, a plate or sheath that can fit just inside the baking pot and hold a weight. I have used a soufflé dish with a salad plate for pressing. Vicki uses a springform pan with a dinner plate for pressing; this also makes for easy removal of the finished pâté—you don't have to turn out the pâté, just unsnap the outer ring of the pan. Another option is a loaf pan and a brick wrapped in paper, foil, or plastic. But my favorite cookware for this method is a fish poacher. The steaming rack fits perfectly inside the beautiful oval pan.

SAUCEPANS AND SOUP POTS

Pots and pans for the slow cook and boiling methods require a weighty bottom and a good seal on the lid. If you pick the kind of cookware that travels easily from the stove top into the oven, then you will save many hours of washing dishes. These pans should have oven-proof handles. Consider a 4- to 6-quart soup pot and a 1½-quart and a 3-quart saucepan.

MISCELLANEOUS TOOLS

Bowls for mixing marinades, dips, and spreads can be wood, glass, or ceramic. A food processor or blender is essential for preparing spreads and dips and comes in handy for pâtés and refrying. A food mill or a Mexican *molcajete* and *tejolote* (mortar and pestle) can replace the electrical appliances. Food mills are hand-cranked sieves, pressing the food through holes so small that it comes out smooth. A *molcajete* is a deep bowl made of lava rock. They vary in shape and size. To prepare a molcajete, grind some rice with a drop of oil into the pores with the *tejolote* (the hand tool also made of lava rock). Brush it out and repeat the procedure. Then the edges won't fall into the food you are preparing. This tool is great for crushing seeds and spices.

Also handy is a ginger grater. A typical design has a metal plate with extra fine, extra sharp teeth imbedded into it to prevent the pulp from going through to the other side. Often there is a small cup at the bottom of the plate to catch the valuable ginger juice. After grating the ginger into pulp, squeeze the fiber against the metal cup and collect the ginger juice. One inch of fresh ginger equals about 1 teaspoon of fresh ginger juice.

Wooden and bamboo hand tools allow you to feel the food as it cooks. We don't beat food as a general rule. Cooking in this style is more about assembling ingredients with fire, setting the stage for transformation, and then letting the fire do the job. Cooks who stir the food a lot think they are the ones doing the cooking when, actually, it is the fire and magic of ingredients that perform the alchemical wizardry. Metal utensils tend to be abrasive on plant food. With the exception of a good wire whisk and a flexible spatula, there is no need for metal hand tools.

A pastry brush with bristles of natural fiber allows even and quick spreading of ghee for filo pastry or for any occasion when you don't want to touch the pot while lining it with oil.

A flame tamer (heat diffuser) is important for pressure cooking and slow cooking, especially if your cookware is not especially heavy. I use mine all the time.

BEAN WORKSHEET

Name of Bean _____

Pretreatment _____

First-Stage Method _____

Second-Stage Method _____

Cooking Liquid _____

Salt Seasoning _____

Oil _____

Herbs and Spices _____

Vegetables

    Major vegetables _____

    _____

    Decorative vegetables _____

Miscellaneous _____

INDEX

ABOUT THE AUTHOR

Joanne Saltzman has spent a lifetime integrating cooking and art. She has been working with natural foods for more than twenty years, and in 1983 she founded the School of Natural Cookery to teach the creative process of cooking to home cooks, personal chefs, and other teachers. She is the author of the cookbook *Amazing Grains,* and her cooking column, "The Natural Cook," appears in *Nexus,* a Colorado bimonthly. She lives in Boulder with her four children.

    For information about cooking programs, or to receive a catalogue of fine cookware and special ingredients, phone the School of Natural Cookery at (303) 444-8068.

Dear Readers,

Many of you have expressed an interest in studying the creative process.

The curriculum at the School of Natural Cookery not only guarantees to improve your cooking skills, but it has the potential to change your life.

We now have beautiful accommodations in Boulder to house you for both Winter and Summer cooking courses. Boulder is an easy, beautiful, health conscious city nestled near the Rocky Mountains and is a pleasure to visit.

Our Fundamentals Course is a comprehensive program in both hands-on and demonstration style classes appropriate for all levels from the novice to the professionally minded cook. We also offer advance programs in Personel Chef Training and a Teacher Training for honest people inclined to share the creative process.

WINTER *(Registration due November 15)*

- *Fundamentals Course: pre-requisite for advance courses*
- *5 weeks*
- *Hands-on classes   Monday-Friday*
- *Private room; Live in central Boulder*

SUMMER *(Registration due May 1)*

- *Summer foods and cooking methods*
- *Friday, Saturday, Sunday*
- *Demonstration classes*
- *Dormitory style; Live in mountains*

To inquire further about the School of Natural Cookery (SNC)

Please write to:

**SNC
PO BOX 19466
BOULDER, CO 80308-2466**

Call: **(303) 444-8068**

PS. Many of you have received return mail from the address in Amazing Grains. I apologize for the confusion. The US postal service decided to cancel all the PO box numbers in the station I had been contracting for more than eight years. Please write to me through the publisher if for some reason these numbers don't work. H.J. Kramer Inc., PO BOX 1082, Triburon, CA 94920.